T0278570

the Spiritual Path

EMBARKING *on the* JOURNEY *of a* LIFETIME

LISA KELLY

LOYOLA PRESS.
A JESUIT MINISTRY

LOYOLA PRESS.
A JESUIT MINISTRY

www.loyolapress.com

Cover art credits: JaneHYork/Shutterstock.com; iStock/Getty Images Plus/sbayram/Getty
Images; Justin Fernando/500px/Getty Images Rebecca Gay.
Backcover author photo: Catherine Kelly

ISBN: 978-0-8294-5871-8
Library of Congress Control Number: 2024942654

Published in Chicago, IL
Printed in the United States of America
24 25 26 27 28 29 30 31 32 33 LSC 10 9 8 7 6 5 4 3 2 1

Dedicated to Jinny Ditzler and all my
fellow pilgrims.

Net proceeds from *The Spiritual Path*
go to La Storta, Pascal's Pantry,
and other non-profit organizations.

Table of Contents

Letter to My Readers

I once visited the rooms where St. Ignatius had lived and died, rooms that have been preserved at the Church of the Gesù in Rome. There, behind glass, I gazed upon the well-worn leather shoes of St. Ignatius you see on the cover of this book. I imagined these shoes carrying St. Ignatius all over Europe as he shared the Spiritual Exercises and established the Jesuits. After all his writings that I had read and all the years of practicing his methods for coming to know God, I had considered Ignatius so far beyond where I could ever be. But somehow in seeing those shoes, St. Ignatius suddenly became a man named Íñigo who referred to himself as "the pilgrim" and who wrote about his life as a journey with God.

And then my gaze fell to my own ratty sneakers. While they would never be worthy of being kept under glass, they did serve the same function of carrying me on my journey. In that instant, though I had been on pilgrimage for a week, for the first time I saw myself as a fellow pilgrim, one who seeks God through a physical and spiritual journey on this earth. I realized that once I saw myself as a pilgrim, the pilgrimage would never end. I will always be seeking to serve God better, to respond to new invitations from God, to be awed by what lies around the bend, and to savor the journey.

As a pilgrim, I am one who is dependent on the kindness of strangers for provision and on fellow travelers for companionship and directions. Rather than needing to rise above others as our culture so often encourages us to do, I need to walk with them. I am so grateful for all my fellow pilgrims—including *you*![1]

You are about to embark on a journey, an adventure, and, ultimately, a pilgrimage. For thousands of years, people have understood a pilgrimage to be a physical journey of the body that animates the spiritual journey of their heart. Similarly,

The Spiritual Path offers a powerful goal-setting process that will guide your actions over the coming months to animate *your* spiritual journey.

There are many different spiritual paths in this life. This particular Spiritual Path process integrates the tools of Ignatian spirituality with a ten-question planning process that has been proven by individuals and organizations over decades. Through multiple invitations to engage the Spirit, you will discern your own unique spiritual path. The process honors your history, context, strengths, and deepest desires. At the end lies a practical one-page Spiritual Path plan (see Page 228) to map your journey for each month. *The Spiritual Path* offers a guide for individuals, couples, or teams to discern new goals year after year as collaborators with the Spirit. It is inspirational, relational, and practical.

St. Ignatius notes, "There are very few people who realize what God would make of them if they abandoned themselves into His hands and let themselves be formed by His grace." *The Spiritual Path* is your invitation to do just that.

Thank you for joining me on this journey, and welcome to the pilgrimage of your life!

About Ignatian Spirituality

While *The Spiritual Path* uses Ignatian language and themes, do not expect this journey to be a deep dive into Ignatian spirituality. The deep dive into Ignatian spirituality would be the *Spiritual Exercises of St. Ignatius of Loyola*, which is a thirty-day retreat offering a process for surrendering one's life to God. The retreat is usually done only once or twice in a lifetime. Even in the 1500s Ignatius knew it wasn't possible for most laypeople to withdraw from the demands of daily life for thirty days, so he added a footnote, number nineteen to be exact, so that the Spiritual Exercises could be done over several months at home while also continuing the demands of daily life. This Retreat in Daily Life might be considered the mid-pool dive into Ignatian spirituality. A person might complete this retreat a few times in their lives. As an Ignatian Associate, I spent two years in ongoing formation, praying through this Retreat in Daily Life version of the Spiritual Exercises, and even twenty years later I'm still fumbling to grasp the fullness of its depths.

This Spiritual Path process is a much less intense way to recognize God's presence within our heart's desires. Think of it as wading into the pool of spirituality from the zero-depth entry rather than diving into the deep end. If you can't conceive of withdrawing for a thirty-day retreat, or the idea of sitting in conversation with a Higher Power is completely foreign to you, this book may be the perfect way to dip your toes into the waters of spirituality. For anyone comfortable swimming in the depths of Ignatian spirituality by going on a thirty-day or eight-day annual retreat, this book offers a clear way to bring the gifts of those experiences back into daily life.

The Colloquy

Often people have a sense that prayer must be a formal recitation of words found in a prayer book written by someone else. On the other end of the spectrum are people thinking the stream of consciousness thoughts that run through our heads all day long are a prayer that only God can hear. A colloquy is in the middle of this spectrum. It is a more dedicated time where you are attentive to being in the presence of God, sharing in your own words and from your own inner experience, and then also listening. In a colloquy you leave space for what God has to say back to you in the thoughts or sensations that emerge from within you. A colloquy is not just a reflection but also a serious discussion about a specific matter. The Spiritual Path process invites you to thirty-five colloquies, each of which builds on the previous one and deepens your relationship with God. Ignatius suggested that people imagine Jesus sitting in an empty chair in their rooms when they pray, and imagine the tone of his voice when he speaks to them, just as happens when two friends talk with each other. I invite you to have these colloquies as if you were talking with any walking partner on a long hike or pilgrimage. Rather than repeating rote prayers, the colloquy practice makes this your unique journey with God.

A Structured Approach to Faith and Action

For St. Ignatius, spirituality and organizational structure went hand in hand. Most of his years as the first leader and administrator of the Jesuits (the largest order of priests in the Catholic Church) were spent writing the *Spiritual Exercises* and the *Constitutions* that established how the Society of Jesus would function. Both works read like user manuals for a faith practice rather than inspirational prayer resources. Thankfully, this structured approach to living and practicing a faith allowed Ignatian spirituality to take root and continue to be practiced for more than five hundred years throughout the world. In a similar way, this step-by-step Spiritual Path process feels more structured than traditional prayer resources or spiritual guides. In the *Spiritual Exercises*, the *Constitutions*, and this book, *The Spiritual Path* (not that these are in any way on the same level!), the focus is on not the process but rather what is experienced and learned in its use. Rather than bristle at the corporate or business-like tools of the Spiritual Path process, consider that the need for clear structure and process reflects Ignatius's own advised way of proceeding toward your desired future.

PART 1

PREPARING FOR THE JOURNEY

Chapter 1

Why Walk the Spiritual Path?

*This left his understanding so very enlightened that he felt
as if he were another man with another mind.*

Ignatius of Loyola

Planning for Your Spiritual Life

Some people are natural-born planners while others jump into an activity with
little to no forethought and go with the flow. Subconsciously though, chances
are that some view of the future is percolating in their minds. We are told to start
planning to pay for our children's college education the day they are born. When
we ask ten-year-olds what they want to be when they grow up, we assume they are
already dreaming about their future. By our mid-teens we are expected to have
plans for future work and how to live independently. Wedding plans can be more
detailed than the Normandy Invasion, covering everything from banners pulled
by overhead planes to the color of nail polish on each finger. We are asked, perhaps
inappropriately, when or if we plan to have children. And beginning with the first
paycheck, we are counselled to plan for retirement. Beyond these major life plans,
there are more immediate plans that must be made: dinner every night, the family
budget, how you will spend your time on any given day. And, the holy grail of all
planning tools, plan your day calendars! Hour by hour, it is easy to plan for all
aspects of your life. So why not plan for your spiritual life?

All those event plans and financial plans and daily plans are helpful and
encouraged for a reason. Planning often takes uncertainty and fear out of the
way. Planning gives you information and insight into what might or might not
be possible. Planning identifies priorities and ensures you stay focused on what
you identify as important. Planning is motivating, giving you something to look

forward to and a reason to do the small tasks required before the larger goal can be met. Planning prevents wasting time. Planning gives you a sense of control.

Aye, there is the rub. Trying to plan our faith lives comes off to some people as if we are trying to control God in a world where we are conditioned to believe that God is supposed to be in control. We often hear the phrase *God has a plan for you*, but that is usually trotted out when someone is totally at a loss about what is happening to them. God's plan is shrouded in mystery, and we are told to keep plodding along because it will all work out in the end. Note: in that scenario, there is nothing expected of us other than belief. We just sit in the centrifuge while life, at God's orchestration, happens to us.

Do you really believe that God is in control of everything and everyone, and all of us are simply acting out some predestined metaphysical drama? If not, then what *is* in God's control? Often, people turn to faith as a *reaction* when bad things happen. Rarely do we *proactively plan* to manifest our faith. Planning for your spiritual life is not about being in control of God, or trying to use some magical power of God to get what you want, but about being intentional in how you *collaborate with* God. As you will come to see, when we are on the Spiritual Path, we are not seeking a sense of control but rather a sense of being in relationship with God.

Enter St. Ignatius of Loyola

According to St. Ignatius of Loyola, people ought to seek God in all things, meaning not in objects, but in all people, places, times, and experiences in their lives.[2] God was not to be found only in the great cathedrals of Europe or in the sacred city of Jerusalem or through the ritual acts performed by clergy. Instead, Ignatius, a layperson with no religious education, encountered God in a most intimate way while confined to his bed in his family's castle in Spain, recovering from a cannonball injury. He came to understand not only that God *could* be available to people in all places and times, but also that God *is* actively, constantly present in all places for all people. In fact, the whole of Ignatian spirituality as handed down over five hundred years is based not on our seeking God but on our being aware that God is constantly seeking us. Not just in church on Sunday. Not only through a priest. Not only in sacramental ceremonies. But in every moment of our lives. Infinite Love reaches out to us in all things, in all experiences, in our deepest desires at each moment to come to wholeness, to know peace, to be comfortable in our own skin.

So if Ignatius is right, and if God really is in all things, then wouldn't God also be in a planning process?

Reframing Success

Translating a traditional goal-setting process into the Spiritual Path hinges on how we define success. Is success a matter of productivity—how much we get done? Is it a matter of quality—how outcomes are rated according to some third-party measurement? Is success reaching a certain financial goal or level of physical achievement or social status? Any of these are legitimate goals for a successful year in a traditional personal plan. But St. Teresa of Calcutta speaks to the heart of the issue in saying, "We aren't called to be successful; we're called to be faithful." Success in many forms is promoted, lauded, and considered the goal of life by many in western culture, where success is symbolized by the car you drive, the house you own, the clothes you wear, the number of commas in your bank balance, and the accolades you receive. This is the worldliness that Pope Francis often calls out for scrutiny. But faith has a different standard. Faith is the domain of the heart. It is often countercultural and is criticized as silly or naive more than it is lauded. It is symbolized by the person you are, the relationships you sustain, the worldview you hold, and the actions you take. Five hundred years ago, Ignatius wrote, in so many words, that success in this life is not about living a long life, being wealthy, healthy, or even honorable, but about being authentic and faithful to who you are created to be. This is where St. Ignatius turned my world upside down many years ago.

In the *Spiritual Exercises*, St. Ignatius offers a clearly stated purpose for living. He writes, "God created human beings to praise, reverence, and serve God, and by doing this, to save their souls."

That sentence is the opening line of the First Principle and Foundation, the heart of Ignatian spirituality. It definitively states both why each person is created and the ultimate goal of this life, which is to save our souls. What it means to save our souls and exactly how to do so is the arena of all spirituality. As far back as the Ten Commandments and the Code of Hammurabi, humans have had prescriptive lists of how to fulfill their purpose. Christianity, birthed from Judaism, brought the understanding of relationship with God and others to this arena based on the lived example and teachings of Jesus. Ignatius's contribution, to spend the whole of our lives in "praise, reverence, and [service of] God" takes some unpacking.

My Journey

When I first started going to spiritual direction as an Ignatian Associate, I had a narrow understanding of what it means to praise and reverence God.[3] In fact, I outright told my spiritual director I just wasn't good at that sort of thing. I imagined praising and reverencing to be the hands raised and swaying in the air at charismatic renewals I had more commonly witnessed with Protestant friends or the solemn hours on knees spent in convents of old. My brilliant spiritual director, a seventy-something, gray-haired, no-nonsense Servite sister, smiled and asked, "How do the lilies of the field praise God?" I fumbled for an answer. "Well, they look pretty. They are just naturally beautiful, and they smell good, and they are just . . . lilies," I pieced together, thinking to myself, *I am no lily!* I couldn't just spend my day blowing in the wind with my face toward the sun. "So, lilies praise God just by being lilies, by being exactly what they were created to be," she explained with a broad smile that reflected knowledge far beyond anything I could fathom. My face remained blank, not understanding how that made any difference to what I needed to do to save my soul. She added, "Whatever you are *uniquely* created and called to be, that is how you praise and reverence God."

I let that revelation just wash over me, feeling relieved that I didn't have to be a lily. There would be no charismatic, arms in the air, "hallelujah" shouting revivals in my future (not that there is anything wrong with that—they just aren't me!). The main purpose of my life was gracefully simple: be fully me. God's deepest desire, God's calling to me, was for me to embrace being me, not to be someone else's version of holy. Why, after sixteen-plus years of Catholic education, had I never grasped this expression of faith? I had memorized lists of commandments to keep, virtues to embrace, and saints to emulate. As helpful as these were, they missed something essential: being aware of and honest about what was churning inside of me. How could I praise and reverence God using my gifts, capacities, personality quirks, and heartfelt desires? I could save my soul by being intentional about my identity as a wife and mother of young children, a peacemaker, a person who loves to laugh, develop programs, and write reflections about faith. Salvation isn't about fulfilling some cosmic formula for moral perfection. It is about living intentionally exactly where I am, nurturing my best self, my truest self.

Praising, reverencing, and serving God to save our souls is less about following preordained rituals or fitting into a prescribed box of what it means to be a good Christian. It is more about honestly naming those things that give our souls wings and those things that drag us down because they don't encourage our best selves. That's where God is in all things. The Ignatian understanding of success is to seek God in every relationship, situation, and moment. God is constantly calling to me, inviting me to be who I am capable of being, even when it is difficult or countercultural. When I discern and choose to be that best me, the me that reflects my faith in an unconditionally loving God, step-by-step I move deeper into relationship with God. And there is always an invitation to go deeper. There is always an invitation to choose the best me in the next moment. There is always another step to take in the journey. And there are always human imperfections and unhealthy desires that draw me away from that best me.

This First Principle and Foundation is our shared Big, Hairy, Audacious Goal.[4] Not just one on a list of goals, but the entirety of the reason for discerning our goals. It begs us to answer two questions specifically and uniquely for ourselves: Given a desire to save my soul, how can I develop as a loving person, and how do I deepen my awareness of God's Spirit within me? The secret Ignatian sauce to answer these questions is that *everything* has the potential to develop and deepen our relationship with God if we are open to the experience as an invitation to do so.

Using the Spiritual Path process to plan the upcoming year does not guide a person to goals that reflect traditional notions of success such as profitability or accumulation. Rather, it sets you up for a year of growing intentionally, systematically, and faithfully into the most authentic version of yourself, into a person who cultivates their gifts and talents in service to others and their experience of God. In following the Spiritual Path, success is being faithful to the person you are created to be and learning to co-labor, or collaborate, with God, the Power of Infinite Love.

Planning Grounded in Discernment and Trust

In addition to changing the orientation of success, two other important adaptations ground this planning process firmly in a faith perspective: discernment and trust. Similar to how decision-making would be used to help map out a traditional plan, *discernment* is a crucial practice in drafting a Spiritual Path. Every individual uses some process for figuring out what direction they are going. Big data has become a huge player in many circles for identifying what direction an organization is going. In some cases, the numbers alone determine success and, consequently, direction and action. Individuals may use pro-and-con lists and rightly consider the numbers and facts of a situation when making a decision. Ignatius recognized that while such external information is valuable in any course of action, the invitations to be our best selves are more likely found through discernment.

Discernment is the art of recognizing and articulating the *healthy desires* of our hearts. It is both a grace and a practice. The joy of Ignatian spirituality is recognizing that those desires you hold in your heart, the deep ones, the ones that you lie awake at night on the edge of sleep dreaming about, really matter. Even the desires that others might think are a little crazy are important. They can bring you joy, energy, peace, and a sense of wholeness by just imagining them. All of these desires can be God calling and inviting you to be who you were created to be. Discerning those healthy desires is how you praise and reverence and serve God, and ultimately save your soul from shriveling up in a cold world whose idea of success is often the exact opposite of what fulfills us or what God is inviting us to be and do with our gifts.

Best-selling author Jim Manney defines discernment as "a state of reflective awareness of the spiritual significance of things."[5] In *The Discerning Heart: Exploring the Christian Path*, authors Wilkie Au and Noreen Cannon Au write, "Discernment refers to both a posture and a process."[6] For me, discernment is something that occurs not just during intentional prayer times, but moment by moment in everyday life. Discernment requires being constantly aware of aligning ourselves with God's view. This involves being open to the possibilities or invitations to respond to the love that each moment holds as well as actively seeking and engaging the Spirit to influence our decisions, including setting goals and planning daily activities. Discernment is a gift that comes from God's initiative. What we are discerning is God's work within ourselves. In his Spiritual Exercises, St. Ignatius offers several methods for discerning the heart's desire, a few of which are incorporated into the Spiritual Path process. Discernment requires an awareness of emotions as well as a brutal self-honesty that Ignatius called spiritual freedom. It means being free from destructive thought patterns and unhealthy desires. Practicing discernment and being honest about the deep desires of your heart is crucial to the Spiritual Path process and to being your authentic self, the person you were created to be. If you are new to discernment, this book is a great tool to begin the practice.

Planning grounded in faith also requires a sense of trust in Something beyond us being at work in the process. Traditional personal goal setting requires a well-spring of motivation. "Believe in yourself!" is the mantra of many a life coach. Affirmation journals, personal coaching insights, and tools for goal tracking are very helpful. But this process isn't about you believing in yourself. Rather, it is about acknowledging that God believes in you. The deepest desires of your heart to grow into a life you feel called to are God's deepest desires for you as well. The Spiritual Path reframes planning from being about me and my future to goal setting being about us, that is God and me, and our future. If Saint Ignatius was indeed right that there is a Force of Infinite Love at work in all aspects of our lives, then that Force is most definitely at work in planning and reaching our goals. That Force is not magic. That Force is not a puppeteer in control of everything that happens on the journey. Trusting in God does not mean the outcome we desire is guaranteed or even easy. Trusting in God means that we are not the only force at work in this endeavor. Trust means we do not walk our spiritual path alone but rather as a collaborator, a member of a team.

Being a Co-laborer with God

In his book *Soar! Build Your Vision from the Ground Up*, author T. D. Jakes has a great understanding of being a co-laborer with God.[7] He points out that God never made a pencil or a computer or directly wrote a song or business plan. God never discovered a medicine or picked up trash or figured out that olives taste really good when stuffed with garlic. God breathed life into humanity and gave us every element on the periodic table and basically said, "Let's play." Whatever good you do in your life, whatever love you share, you are co-laboring with God. But God didn't just set everything in motion once and walk away. God continues to constantly be saying, "Let's play! Let's create! Let's build!" It is in that co-laboring that we individually grow, allowing God to work through our gifts and talents to be ever present in everyday life just as much as at the moment of creation. That is true for you as well; you were not created just once but are continually being re-created through every interaction with this life force that we call God.

God has given us not only life and consciousness but also a will free to choose how to use this one body, this one era, these breaths. Along the path of life, every day in fact, there are invitations to orient your life toward that Infinite Love and wholeness or away from that Infinite Love toward emptiness. Those invitations don't come to you only from outside yourself. They also come from the Spirit within, from the healthy longings or desires of your heart. Ignatius recognized that those desires for goodness, love, justice, and wholeness were God's personal invitations to us to be co-laborers with God in this precious life we have been given. In *The Way of Discernment*, Elizabeth Liebert writes, "There exists in us a genuine ability to co-create with God our particular futures as well as to contribute to the collective future of our communities, and indeed, of everything living on earth."[8] Together with God we discern what might be possible for our lives over the coming months.

Invitations to be a co-laborer with God can change throughout a lifetime. They are understood as vocational callings, but also as opportunities in the moment, any moment, to reflect the love of God in this world through your unique capacities, passions, and situations. By reflecting that love, you grow more fully into the person you are called to be. A person may have a specific vocation to marriage or religious life or single life, but even within those vocations there are invitations to co-labor in how you live out that vocation. As a member of a European religious order, St. Teresa of Calcutta spoke of her desire to go to India as having "a call within a call." She experienced yet another call within a call to serve the poorest of the poor after having taught for many years at a private all-girls school in India. An invitation to be a co-laborer with God may invite you to use your gifts in places far outside your comfort zone. It might require you to partner with others. For some people, an invitation to be a co-laborer may take off in their heart like a Porsche on a wide open freeway; for others, the invitation may be more like a slow Sunday drive just exploring what might be possible; for still others, the calling may feel more like being stuck in an L.A. traffic jam, given cultural or personal barriers that stand in the way. The invitation may also address something that is aching in your heart or nagging at your conscience. No one knows the exact route of your spiritual path. In fact, half the joy of the journey is being surprised at what is possible when you are walking beside God, discerning new invitations to be a collaborator all along the way.

Who Is God for You?

Seeing yourself as a co-laborer with God is easier when you have a clear name and conception of God in your head. A cursory review of familiar religious texts and Scripture reveals dozens of names and titles for God. They offer Jehovah, Elohim, Allah, Adoni, Father, Creator, Jesus, Christ, Messiah, the Way, Wisdom, the Door, Dayspring, the Almighty, the Alpha and the Omega, Holy Spirit, Holy One, King of kings, Lord, Abba, Redeemer, Savior, Shepherd, Beloved, and many more. All of them seem hopelessly inadequate, knowing there can be no limiting names put on that which is unlimited. God identifies as "I Am" to Moses, perhaps less of a name and more the totality of existence. Beloved American Franciscan spirituality teacher Richard Rohr, OFM, explains that *Yahweh* is meant not to be a name but to be the act of breathing, of life itself: *Yah* on the inhale and *weh* describing the exhale.[9] Aristotle referred to God as an action, more verb than noun. Alcoholics Anonymous refers to and relies upon "a Higher Power as we understand it." A fellow Ignatian Associate who did the Spiritual Exercises for the first time in her seventies often talked in our faith sharing group about her adventures and conversations with Sam. It was only after a few months that I realized Sam was not her former husband or grown son but her name for the Holy Spirit! The common denominator is not what we call this God of many names, but what is our experience of this God. Is it infinite, unconditional, overwhelming, forgiving, healing, joy-filled, agapic love? Or is it something totally different?

For this Spiritual Path journey, I refer to God most often as your Walking Partner. Through every part of the coming journey, your Walking Partner will be with you to inspire you, encourage you, free you from fears, celebrate with you, and sometimes even carry you. Jesus on the road to Emmaus in the Gospel of Luke was the Walking Partner to the two apostles whose hearts burned within them (see Luke 24:13–35).

Everyone on the Spiritual Path retreats relates differently to their Walking Partner and is comfortable with a different representation. Some people imagine Jesus sitting in the chair next to them and putting on his hiking boots too. Another participant imagined a hat that looked like a halo and embodied the Spirit. For some people, their companion on this journey is Saint Ignatius, or a former friend, mentor, parent, or spouse who has died. One fellow pilgrim imagined carrying Yoda on his back, just the way Luke Skywalker carried Yoda in *Star Wars*! This is your hike. You are free to personify your Walking Partner in any way that allows you to be your best self and bring you peace.

Before you begin this journey, however, it is vital that you hold a healthy image of God. Medieval images of an old man with a long white beard often standing in harsh judgment and waiting to punish missteps cannot fill us with the depth of love required to courageously love others. In fact, such a fearful image can do harm by spreading fear rather than forgiveness, mercy, and love.

Just as you would be advised to not undertake a strenuous hike if your body isn't healthy, take time now to work with a spiritual director to be sure your understanding of God is healthy.

Me? A Co-laborer? I Don't Think So

Over the years I have heard many excuses people have for not claiming their identity as co-laborers or being intentional about setting goals spiritually by making a Spiritual Path plan.

Being a co-laborer sounds like I am trying to be equal with God. Jesus himself did not think equality with God was something to be grasped (see Philippians 2:6). Seeing ourselves as collaborators is about listening to God, allowing God to work through us, and accepting that we have within us the *capacity* to follow God's will. Anything you do in this life that enhances your life and the lives of others is co-laboring with God.

This sounds really inspiring, but there is no way I have time to add one more thing to my plate. Is there not enough time in your life to affirm that you are on the right track? This is *your* lifetime. Is it your heart's desire for you to be too busy to take time for yourself? If not, then that is not God's desire for you either. Saying you don't have time to be intentional about what you are doing and why is like someone on a train saying, "It doesn't matter where this train is going, I just need to stay on this train." If your life is really on the right track right now, busy as it may be, going through a reflection process to articulate and hold yourself accountable to this trajectory only enhances and reaffirms your resolve. But if, just if, there are areas of your life that are off track from where you are called, wouldn't it be better to make those course corrections as soon as possible? This is not adding another thing to your plate but reflecting on everything that is (and isn't) on your plate right now and where God is at work on that plate! To complete this process thoughtfully and without distraction takes a few hours, at most a weekend retreat to set your goals, and a short check-in at the end of each month. The result is an honest, faith-filled reality check. Most people find it is freeing and affirming to clarify their spiritual path rather than continually juggling directionless tasks.

I gave up on goal setting a long time ago. I am with you on this one. Life is much easier when I just wander aimlessly and wait for the good stuff to happen to me, complaining when it doesn't. This thinking means I don't have to carry the stress of trying to grow and change and reach a goal, nor the humiliation of not reaching it. Goal setting feels like I am just setting myself up for failure. Giving up on goal setting comes from one of two places: laziness or victimization. Either it is easier to do nothing, or I have bought into the belief that I can't change anything. Not even that the world can't change, or others can't change, but *I* can't change. We look to our past failures and mistakes or what others lay on us as our past failures and mistakes as evidence of our worthlessness. We have lost confidence in ourselves.

Enter God. Enter the power of unconditional, divine, forgiving, empowering, Infinite Love. This is where the Spiritual Path process becomes the most unique goal setting experience you have ever had. God never gives up on you. This love does not focus on past mistakes or failures. The Spirit constantly seeks your growth and movement toward fulfillment. God desires to be in the adventure of life with you. It's not all on you. When you collaborate with God to set goals and, in reaching them, grow and change the world around you, your motivation and resolve come from a different place. That doesn't mean there are any guarantees. It just means you have your priorities straight. Thy will be done, not my will to stay safe and unstressed.

I am scared God will call me to something I really don't want to do. Insider tip on spiritual planning: there is something bigger than your fears. Years ago, my husband and I made the crazy leap of faith to move to a developing country with our three children under the age of nine. It required us to learn a new language, leave behind our community and family, risk serious illness, and forget almost every expectation of safety and protection for our children. Seatbelts and car seats? Non-existent. Clean drinking water? Only if we hauled the ten-gallon jug up a long flight of stairs. Lights and electricity to pump water? If we were lucky, on Tuesdays and Thursdays when it was turned on for our section of town. Daily I lived in fear of either physically endangering or at least mentally damaging my own children. While my husband had a sense of being welcomed and embraced by a new community of friends, I had a sense of being chased by zombies I could neither understand nor speak to. It was so hard! Truth be told, I was scared to go, I struggled when I was there, and I was relieved to come home. And now, looking back, I can say without hesitation that experience was the greatest gift we could have given to our children and our own souls. Courage begets courage. Once you face a fear because you are called to something greater, in this case, educating about social justice and living in solidarity with the poor, those fears become your staircase to growing deeper in relationship with God. If your heart's desire really is to be one with God, to be the person you are capable of being, to fulfill your identity as a collaborator with God, then that is bigger than any fear.

What if I fail? Does that mean I have failed God? Thomas Merton got it right when he prayed, "I believe the desire to please you does in fact please you." Failure is never found in not reaching a goal because in trying we are at the very least growing and moving toward the goodness to which we are called. We may not always get there, but we are growing and moving in the right direction. Failure is found only in never trying at all. Walking a spiritual path is not a test to pass or fail, it is a journey to be experienced. At the end of each leg of the journey, you reflect, assess, learn, adapt, and get back up to keep walking. Along the way, you grow in your capacity to discern God's call and your connection with God. In fact, it may be that the intentionality to practice your faith, even more than the particular goal you set, is what you are being called to.

My Journey

During the course of writing this book, my own Spiritual Path plan was ripped to shreds in a matter of minutes. My husband and I had discerned for well over a year that our second half of life, post children at home, was to be in Spain, teaching and working on the Ignatian Camino and at Jesuit schools. I had transitioned out of my job. We had sold our home of twenty years. We had visas and plane tickets and an apartment in Madrid. All of these were goals on my Spiritual Path plan. And then, four weeks before we were set to leave, completely out of the blue, I was diagnosed with stage 4 cancer and given a fifty-fifty chance of being alive within a year, even with the best treatment available. Within minutes of my doctor relaying my diagnosis, I thought of my goals. I learned very quickly that *discernment is not prophecy*. The goals I had discerned did indeed drive me to be the person I wanted to be, but the world around me—including my body—was not in my control.

In walking my Spiritual Path, I learned to trust that God is not just at the end of the journey but is walking every step with me. Having a Spiritual Path plan on paper and having to acknowledge how my new reality impacted the relationships to which I was called kept me going through a season when it was hard to even have the will to live. I had to let go of some goals like being able to have fluent conversations in Spanish or working out at the gym several times a week. I had to face the reality of new goals, including dying with dignity. But when everything else gave way, having this process to fall back on at the end of the day or month gave me some sense of peace in an out-of-control reality. My Spiritual Path plan ensured I prioritized my relationships and took practical actions that matched my limited physical abilities. Most important, it ensured I continued to collaborate with God to transition to whatever comes next.

Since my diagnosis I am more convinced than ever in the power of spirituality and the primacy of relationships in goal setting. When time in this life is limited, those relationships become the priority for everyone. But we need not wait for death to be knocking on our door! Each day is an opportunity to walk a spiritual path, to grow and to let go, and to learn to trust in the power of Infinite Love. I haven't failed God, and God hasn't failed me. Together we have kept walking and growing through the ups and downs of life.

Growing, Growing, Growing, Gone

Hopefully that voice negating your identity as a co-laborer is diminishing as you prepare to discern your Spiritual Path plan. Observe any sense of hope, possibility, excitement, or other emotions welling up within you as you start to embrace this new identity. Those are the invitations, the deep desires, that God places within your heart.

Walking the Spiritual Path will change you. Going through this process, embracing your identity as a co-laborer, discerning, and responding to the invitations before you will require you to face some challenges both within and beyond yourself. By facing these challenges, with God and your fellow pilgrims at your side, you grow, step-by-step, into the person you are created to be. The Spiritual Path, at its core, is a process of growth. Your spiritual path is how you are called to grow now in whatever life situation you find yourself. You will embrace new, healthier behaviors and let go of dysfunctional thinking. In his autobiography, St. Ignatius talks about being taught by God as if he were a schoolboy. St. Irenaeus, a second-century theologian and bishop, taught that the glory of God is the human person fully alive. Growing into that person does not happen magically, nor is it predestined, but it is possible with openness and intentionality on your part.

There are invitations and opportunities for growth in every stage of life. As children, the need to be intentional about learning and growth is required through schooling. As adults, most of our learning comes from experience rather than from books and tests. The gift of maturity is to recognize and admit how much more we need to learn about life and ourselves. I have found the wisest people are often the humblest. The same goes for our faith lives and learning about God. If our understanding and experience of God haven't changed over the years, then we have a lot to learn, especially about being co-laborers.

While I was writing this book, Jinny Ditzler, my inspiration and the woman to whom this book is dedicated, passed away. Her memorial service was a testament to all that she had created (or co-created) in her life, with hundreds of people from four different continents honoring her work and her way of living that had made such an impact on their lives. In *Your Best Year Yet!*, Jinny notes, "What motivates most of us far more than material success or recognition is our desire to be true to ourselves and live our lives in ways that demonstrate our personal values and beliefs."[10] Jinny was still working her annual plan even into the last months of her life. In her final year, she sought to grow and focus her mindset by being intentional about how she lived every day. If she could whisper one thing into your ear right now, I think it would be, "Rather than letting life happen to you, make it happen."[11] Find the path that love would lead.

Finding Your Why for Walking This Spiritual Path

Planning is an important part of all aspects of life, including our spiritual lives. Orienting our lives toward God and discerning who we are called to be must be intentional. In fact, St. Ignatius would say this is the only way to save our souls. We cannot just allow our lives to be blown by the winds of culture, other peoples' agendas, or looming world events and expect to land safely on the shores of the personal paradise we think God has waiting for us. You are called to be a co-laborer with God in this life. The excuses to not be a co-laborer leave you stuck in the muck of the life you are in right now. We have no time to waste. This life is such an amazing journey to share with God, and each of us has a lot of ground to cover before sunset!

This is your first colloquy, or conversation, with your Walking Partner on this Spiritual Path. Put yourself in a shared space with the image of God that brings you peace and safety. Maybe you have known each other for some time and are comfortable with this conversation. Maybe this is your first personal meetup, and these questions feel like small talk. The key is to recognize that this invitation to have a colloquy is not just writing your reflections but actually having a conversation about these things. It is where you begin to get to know your Walking Partner who will be with you for the entirety of this journey.

Colloquy 1: Why Walk the Spiritual Path?

1. Why do I want to make a Spiritual Path plan?

2. How does Ignatius's understanding that we praise God by being authentic to our own deepest desires challenge traditional conceptions of practicing faith?

3. What image or concept of God am I most comfortable with as my Walking Partner?

My Walking Partner's response to what I have shared:

Chapter 2

How to Walk the Spiritual Path

Growth is never by mere chance;
it is the result of forces working together.
James Cash Penney

The Cycle of Growth

In the little-known book *Les Sources de la Paix Intellectuelle* (*The Sources of Intellectual Peace*), published in 1892, French philosopher Léon Ollé-Laprune wrote that each person has "something to do in life" as a co-operator of God.[12] His philosophy for being a "co-operator" was later adopted by Cardinal Joseph Cardijn, founder of the Young Christian Workers, and became the shorthand method for living out social activism known as See, Judge, Act. Cardijn taught this method as an ongoing cycle for the church and its members to continually apply their faith practically in daily life. Under this approach, change or growth happens when those in a situation see the reality of the situation honestly, factually, objectively, and then judge the rightness of the situation in light of Scripture and tradition. The next necessary step is to act upon that reality in a way consistent with their judgment. This method was further adapted by the Catholic Franciscans and the Poor Clares, widely used in Catholic Social Teaching, and reaffirmed in Vatican II documents as the methodology for "responding to the needs of our times."[13] Multiple papal encyclicals and letters, including the writings of Pope Francis, reiterate this method of making faith practical and relevant to daily living. A fourth phase, to reflect on the cycle and learn from the experience, was added prior to beginning the cycle again as part of Ignatian pedagogy.

The See-Judge-Act-Reflect method can bring our faith to bear upon social issues such as systemic poverty and violence, but also on our personal faith lives. In the Spiritual Path, this method is called the Cycle of Growth. It is the cycle of movement toward our horizon. It is the *how* of the Spiritual Path process. Learning *how* to walk a spiritual path helps us to not get lost in a spiritual wasteland of repetitious prayer that does not make room for action and growth. In Ignatian language, it is a *way of proceeding*, and it is never ending.

The Cycle of Growth calls us to continually step outside of the moment at hand to be aware of where we are in the cycle. In *The Constitutions of the Society of Jesus*, St. Ignatius implored his young seminarians to review their day every few hours, seeking to understand where God's invitation had been made to them and how they responded. Buddhist teachings also encourage this idea of stepping outside of our emotional, ego-driven engagement of the moment to observe the dynamics at play. Being conscious of where we are in the Cycle of Growth at any given moment not only allows more space for receiving insight but also frees us from making rash or habitual assumptions, judgments, or responses.

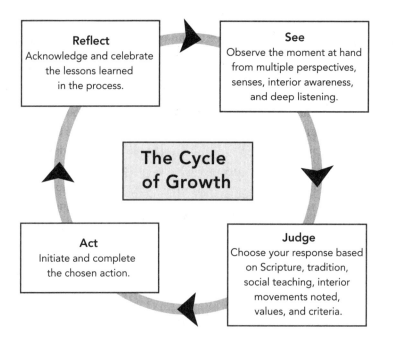

Reflect
Acknowledge and celebrate the lessons learned in the process.

See
Observe the moment at hand from multiple perspectives, senses, interior awareness, and deep listening.

The Cycle of Growth

Act
Initiate and complete the chosen action.

Judge
Choose your response based on Scripture, tradition, social teaching, interior movements noted, values, and criteria.

Think of the Cycle of Growth as a spiral path taking you deeper into relationship with God. Every time you complete a cycle—See-Judge-Act-Reflect—you will learn something new about yourself, your calling, the world around you, or God. Every time you complete a cycle you gain a little more courage or wade a little deeper into this pool of spirituality. Thus, rather than being a journey from point A to point B, the Spiritual Path is a spiral that coils deeper than you ever imagined. Even the mystics will say there is no definitive *there* to get to on our journey to God. Paradoxically there is only deeper and broader, becoming more comfortable in our own skin while at the same time recognizing how we uniquely can give of ourselves to help others. This Spiritual Path is a dynamic journey where

The Spiritual Path is a spiral, practicing the Cycle of Growth again and again throughout the months of the coming year.

we seek both a deeper interior experience of God and a broader outward expression of faith. To become more available to the world is growth! Unfortunately, the notion of a hierarchical, male-centric relationship to God has permeated Christian spirituality; undoing it, by engaging this circle relationship, will take some work.

Indigenous spirituality from thousands of years ago embraced the notion of a circular relationship with a Higher Power at the core. Western philosophers also embraced the notion of a spherical relationship with God, but it was not developed or taught because it didn't reflect the very human-centric hierarchical structure of the church. Thomas Aquinas taught that all of creation goes out from God and ultimately returns to God. Alain de Lille, a professor of theology at the University of Paris in the 1100s, wrote, "God is an infinite sphere, whose center is everywhere, and whose circumference is nowhere."[14] The pilgrimage of your life means walking this spherical relationship with God.

On the Spiritual Path, as you practice the Cycle of Growth in chapters 3–6, you move down the spiral, deeper into your self-reflection and the Spirit within. Chapter 7 reflects the ever-deepening base of your Spiritual Path, how you are uniquely created and gifted by God. In chapters 8–10 you continue practicing the Cycle of Growth moving upward on the spiral, manifesting the Spirit in the world around you. In time you will come to recognize that walking a spiritual path means always being invited to move along this spiral path through another Cycle of Growth where you See-Judge-Act-Reflect daily, monthly, annually. Let's take a closer look at each phase in this cycle.

The Four Phases of the Cycle of Growth

The four phases of the Cycle of Growth are not specific to a set time period. They can happen over a year or in just a few minutes. Some phases may take more time than others, depending on the situation. A person might spend weeks seeing or gathering information about an invitation, including taking time for introspection, and a day to make a judgment and act. One phase may bleed into the next without a clear boundary, but the order is crucial.

The key to working the Cycle of Growth is to know which phase you are in at any moment and to be aware of the pitfalls of that phase. The Spiritual Path process walks through each phase of the cycle several times as you draft your plan, and each month as you continue the journey. Because God is active in each phase, constantly seeking our growth, effort to collaborate with that Presence through the colloquies is vital.

See: Naming the reality that is before you. The hardest part of the See stage is being honest and detached from emotions enough to observe them without jumping to the Judge phase or becoming defensive. Identify only the facts of the moment, including what you don't know. Ask others for input. How others see a situation is an important part of discerning your response. Use your intellect to gain new information. Science is indeed another path to God, not a barrier. If the facts are there, name them.

See is the phase where we ask God to open our eyes to what is most crucial for us to observe at any moment or in any situation. Prayer at this point can simply be, "What am I missing? What is catching my attention?" Although the phase is identified as "See," observation can be made through all our senses—hearing, smelling, touching, tasting, identifying the energy in the space, and connecting with others' emotional auras. This is the phase of being fully present to what is happening around you and within you.

The See phase is also the phase of brainstorming, imagining, and recognizing what is going on inside you as possibilities and insights emerge. Consider your energy, emotion, memory, and visions. Remember, this is not the Judge phase, just the time to articulate. Feelings aren't right or wrong. They just arise. Observing and naming them without judgment is like reading a road sign. Judging whether you want to go down that road requires more information. Anything that comes to you could be an invitation for growth or a possible next step on your path. It could also be a detour. Name those feelings. My spiritual director would tell me to just sit with them, and recognize they are a factual part of the situation. Acknowledging "I am angry about this," "I am scared," "I am excited!" is a reality for you to face and explore for understanding. The fastest way to miss an invitation from God is to discard your feelings as irrelevant or somehow wrong. In this first phase, "see" what has arisen within you. You can judge it later.

My Journey

Our family used this Cycle of Growth process in making a plan to move to El Salvador. The facts we had to name included our children's ages (then eight, twelve, and thirteen) and how another move might affect them. We took seriously the facts of the political situation in the country at the time, the potential career benefits and costs, and the facts of actual benefits and costs to our lives at that moment. Notably, in the See stage it is important to name potential future risks and benefits as openly and honestly as possible without letting fears or desires sway you too much in either direction. Yes, there was a chance of contracting disease, but it was low. Yes, there was political unrest, but we would have locals to help us navigate the situation. In this phase, we talked to people we trusted and asked as many questions as we could to address any fears or allay any concerns, but we honestly named those too. Knowing we were in the first phase of the cycle, we were committed to staying open and observing over time how the invitation played out, especially in our hearts, until we were ready to move to the next phase.

Judge: Choose from the options before you. This is the phase of decision-making with the recognition that because we are co-laborers, the Spirit of God is weighing in through Scripture, tradition, Catholic Social Teaching, community, friendships, and prayerful discernment; it isn't only me deciding what I want for myself in this situation.

Good decision-making is based on first establishing clear *criteria* for any decision. Criteria determine the boundaries within which we can take an action. Criteria are much easier to set and prioritize before a situation reaches the judgment phase or even before seeing what is possible. If an option meets our predetermined criteria, the final decision of what action to take is at least acceptable, if not easy and clear. Only after we take the action, in the third phase, and reflect upon it, in the fourth phase, will there be growth in our understanding of what criteria to establish in the future. Ignatian spirituality adds one clear criteria to all decision-making: I shall choose whichever response better serves God and deepens God's Spirit within me. The art of discernment is giving full consideration to which response would deepen the Spirit within us and move us closer to God. While decision-making is one point in the cycle, or, said another way, takes place during one moment in time, discernment is occurring throughout the entire cycle as we reflect upon the movements of the Spirit within us.

The Judge phase requires honesty about our motivations for the action we are considering. Far too often we practice our faith on the basis of what we *should* do rather than discover and admit the true desires of our heart. Many a spiritual director would advise us not to "should all over ourselves." This isn't about what we should do on the basis of some outside notion of what it means to be a good person. In fact, doing something because we should do it is a recipe for failure and for moving away from God, because resentments and negativity can build up inside. This phase of growth is about discerning what we are being called to do. The invitation may be a challenge, or countercultural, or contrary to our habits, but if we embrace it as a possibility that helps us move toward God, toward a greater reflection of Infinite Love, growth is possible.

Choose actions that give you a sense of wholeness or move you closer to God, even by just trying them. You can't fake your way to wholeness with God, so don't start with what others say you should do to get there. Instead change *should* to *could*. This moves from an expectation held by others or cultural norms to an invitation to growth.

Far too often, the judging phase is given short shrift as a momentary blip on our journey. *Are you doing this? Yes, or no? What's it going to be?* Instead, as you are walking your Spiritual Path, accept the uncertainty and awkwardness of this stage, of not knowing exactly which way you are being called. In prayer, try to name all that you have seen objectively and ask for help reading the map. Tease out what is of God. Call out or bring to light the motivations behind the possible decisions. Discernment is all about getting to the source. In the *Spiritual Exercises*, Ignatius notes that to someone who is moving toward God, the Spirit will give encouragement, strength, and joy, and touch "lightly and sweetly like water on a sponge."[15] The opposite is true for a person moving away from God, perhaps considering doing something unethical, hurtful, dangerous, or contrary to the authenticity of the decision maker. In that case, St. Ignatius counsels, it is the Spirit of God that enters our thoughts with "stings of conscience and remorse," and "clamor, contrariness, and unruliness" that will not let go of our hearts. The spirit *not* of God, however, enters "quietly though an open door," through our weakest point, to bring self-gratification and disordered pleasure, often to be kept secret. The spirit *not* of God will bring discouragement and sadness by proposing problems, erecting roadblocks, and fomenting anxiety. That awkward time of judging which way the winds are blowing can be a blessed and sacred space for experiencing real connection to God. Uncertainty is a space where there is room for the Spirit of God to speak to your heart.

Finally, the Judge phase includes being aware of the aftermath of the decision. If the decision, once made, weighs heavy on the heart or leads to unforeseen consequences, reconsideration is called for.

My Journey

For our discernment to go to El Salvador or not, we had to trust Ignatius's second way of proceeding and be honest, given the facts and our feelings while looking at two potential futures. One invitation took the family out of the country again for another six months, giving up my position as an executive director of a nonprofit while promising many of the stresses of living overseas that we had experienced in the Dominican Republic. The other invitation was to stay home for those six months and continue to serve as we were, allowing the children to continue traditional schooling. The question was, which invitation brought us a greater sense of moving toward God or responding to an invitation to growth? Which reflected our criteria of better serving God, given our calling as parents and professionals? We discerned to accept that invitation, noting that after it was made, in the months leading up to our leaving, we continued, for the most part, to feel excitement and assurance that it was the right decision.

Act: This is what you do or don't do or say in a given situation. You act only after going through the See and Judge phases. Keep in mind that even non-action or discerning not to act is indeed an action that can move you toward or away from God. If you spend your life seeing and judging but never following through with concrete action, you will be living in your head and moving no closer to God. Faith without works is dead (see James 2:26). You may spend hours planning your year of living your faith, but if it ends up on a shelf in the folder labeled "Someday I'll Get to That," have you really grown closer to the person you are called to be? Ignatian spirituality is rooted in the mantra of being contemplatives in action. You are going through all of this to do something, not to just sit on the sidelines of life. In the *Contemplation on Divine Love*, St. Ignatius says, "Love ought to manifest itself more by deeds than by words."[16] Connection to God is often experienced during this phase in the gifts of courage, patience, discipline, and persistence. According to spiritual director Ruth Leacock, "Much of our hesitation to take an action can be eliminated simply by moving from an 'I can' or an 'I can't' perspective to a 'God, use me' perspective."[17]

An action can require just a few seconds of time or years of life. If we fail to initiate or complete the action in the time set to do it, the cycle moves on to the next phase. In the Spiritual Path process, there is no stopping in any one phase for long. Time limits and accountability mechanisms ensure the Cycle of Growth is always moving. Without these, we can claim to be walking a spiritual path, but really, we are only going through the motions, and no real progress is happening.

My Journey

The action of moving to El Salvador for my husband's sabbatical brought both joy and challenges. My daughter found herself almost a year behind in math compared to other students in the European school in which we enrolled the kids, and she struggled to find other friends who could communicate in English, so books became her lifelong companion. My sons enjoyed almost rock star status as the only Spanish-speaking blue-eyed boys among a class of very friendly Salvadoran teenage girls. I was able to study and build connections with people at the University of Central America, one of the holiest sites in all of Ignatian spirituality, given the UCA martyrs who taught and were killed there in 1989. My husband made a life-changing connection to martyr Rutilio Grande, SJ, while researching his personal homilies and writings. But the realities of the political situation were also ever-present. We saw and witnessed the aftermath of people being murdered too many times, to the point where we could no longer deny what we were seeing and had to name that fact, which brought us home early for our own safety.

Reflect: The fourth phase of the Cycle of Growth is where most of the learning and growth takes place. The Reflect phase is where we acknowledge and celebrate. Did we follow through on the action and complete it? What did we learn along the way? Where was God in all this?

That question "Where was God in all this?" summons us to look back over all three phases in the light of God's presence and grace. Hindsight truly offers clarity. Ignatius taught that the aftermath of thoughts, feelings, and actions is a key part of the whole discernment process. If the aftermath leaves us with a bad taste in our mouth, it is likely that the initial discernment was not of God. If the aftermath leaves us with a sense of peace, maybe we did all we could or acted the right way, even if it seemed that the world was against us, then the judgment and subsequent action were likely of God as well.

Taking time to celebrate victories and to acknowledge failures or short-comings is vital. The Reflect phase is notably not the Judge phase. This is not meant to be a time of inflating or deflating the ego. Healthy accountability is not about punishment or even guilt. Accountability is first and foremost for motivation and should be about forgiveness and learning from our weak-nesses only in the event of inaction. This phase gives us the opportunity to reassess, make adjustments, and go at it again. Most importantly, reflection, celebration, and acknowledgment reinvigorate our spiritual journey even if it leads to a new direction. That is growth. The Reflect phase is also where we look ahead and imagine future steps we are being called to take as the Cycle of Growth begins again.

My Journey

Reflecting on our months in El Salvador taught my husband and I so much about our faith. Were we wrong in our original discernment to go because we had to leave early for safety reasons? Absolutely not! We were inspired by the spirit of the University of Central America and by Rutilio Grande, SJ, to give even more than we imagined to the causes of justice and the fight against oppression. We bonded closer as a family, knowing our kids now had tools to deal with so many challenging situations of adolescence from a more worldly perspective. We experienced God in new friendships and the experience of solidarity with those living on the margins. Most important, we returned with new perspectives on how to see the present moment we were being invited into.

I Think We Have a Flat!

This Cycle of Growth is the way to practice being a co-laborer with God. Some phases of the cycle will be harder than others. People get stuck in different phases. In our monthly reflections, anyone in our group is free to call out, "Looks like you've got a flat!" In other words, the cycle is not rolling.

- Some people have trouble with the first phase, just seeing reality or the facts before them. They cling to a myopic way of seeing life and are therefore stuck in how they respond.
- Some people are quick to jump to the Judge phase. Without engaging the Spirit, they judge themselves as lacking, they judge others as not worthy, or judge that nothing can be done. Some people are paralyzed by having to make a decision and instead procrastinate, perhaps by obsessively seeking more information.
- Some people get stuck in the Act phase. They know exactly what they are called to do but don't follow through. It all sounds good, but something more pressing gets in the way.
- More often than not, the fourth phase is skipped entirely. Who has time to sit and reflect? We need to keep acting! There is another deadline to be met! Another goal to be achieved. What is wrong with that? Burnout. No growth. Nothing learned. Mistakes or misconceptions repeated. You miss seeing God in clear hindsight. The fourth phase is where you benefit from the entire experience.

Practicing the Cycle of Growth

The Spiritual Path process embeds the Cycle of Growth so you can experience how it is applied. You will be asked to see an aspect of your own life as a detached observer, then judge or make a decision about what you have seen. For now, the Act phase is writing and committing to your one-page Spiritual Path plan that is at the back of the book. That act of writing is sacred and a symbolic act of commitment and acknowledgment of your heart's deepest desires. The words you put down will be your map for the coming year. Like a marriage license or any other written symbolic act, articulating your Spiritual Path is the start of a new orientation of life lived out daily. While there is no magic in the act, there is power to the extent you freely embrace the commitment. Each cycle ends with an opportunity to reflect on your experience of going through that Cycle of Growth, acknowledging what stirred inside as you acted by writing out your Spiritual Path, and celebrating your efforts! After you draft your Spiritual Path plan at the end of this book, each month of the coming year offers another opportunity to repeat and practice the Cycle of Growth. You begin with monthly goal setting and end with monthly acknowledgment and celebration. The more you practice, the more readily you can identify which phase you are in and how to keep moving on your spiritual path. The beauty of the Cycle of Growth is its continuous nature. The end of the Spiritual Path is not a brick wall but rather a new horizon filled with invitations from God for you to again take the next step as a co-laborer.

Forces of Nature at Work on Your Spiritual Path

As you become more comfortable with the Cycle of Growth, and as you become more accustomed to using a Spiritual Path plan, putting faith into action becomes easier and allows you to make progress toward your goals. Richard Rohr, OFM, talks about the journey this way: "We are created with an inner drive and necessity that sends all of us looking for our True Self, whether we know it or not. This journey is a spiral and never a straight line."[18] There is an amazing parallel in the natural world to the phenomenon you are about to experience.

In the laws of physics, whenever an object completes a rotation or a cycle, there is an actual force at work: centripetal force. Centripetal means center-seeking. Your center is your Higher Power, and this life is not just about you trying to get to God but about God actively pulling you closer. Pulling you in. You will not be going in circles to end where you began. Life is a vortex that pulls you into *a way of being* that you can't escape. It becomes how you experience your days, your weeks, your years.

But there is something amazing about the centripetal-force analogy of using the See-Judge-Act-Reflect cycle as your method of movement on your faith journey: complementing the *centripetal force* that draws us deeper into our center, there is a *centrifugal force* which is the equal and opposite reaction to the centripetal force. This force pulls us outward beyond ourselves. In other words, this is not a naval-gazing exercise where you spend the next year living in such a way that you are thinking only about yourself. As you are pulled inward to a deeper relationship with God, the only possible equal and opposite reaction is to expand and act upon the world beyond yourself. The more you grow toward your center—which is to say your best self, the person you were created to be, the reflection of God you alone can embody—the more you will exert that force of love on others and on the world around you. Walking a spiritual path will never be to save only your own soul because the way we save our souls is through loving others and the world around us. The centripetal force pulls you in as you grow closer to your Higher Power while the centrifugal force pushes you outside of yourself in service to others in equal measure. The first few questions on the Spiritual Path will start building that center-seeking force within you. The questions that frame your actual goal-setting are powered by that centrifugal outward-seeking force.

Grab That Trail Map

The ultimate horizon of an Ignatian spiritual path is the Principle and Foundation, which is to praise, reverence, and serve God by being the person I am called to be, and am capable of being, in my given time and context, and in so doing to save my soul.

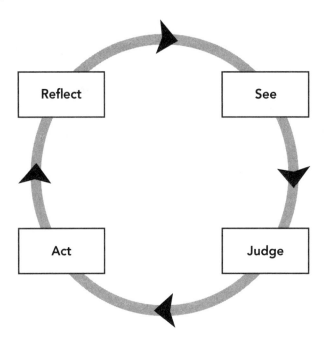

Through the journey of this book, you are going to map a path to that horizon using the Cycle of Growth. The scenic overlooks of this pilgrimage include:

- articulating lessons to make your spiritual journey smoother;
- creating a Sacred Mantra, a faithful internal compass;
- identifying your unique Sources of Energy for this journey;
- discerning your goals and completing a one-page Spiritual Path plan; and
- committing to the first steps on that path over the coming month and the tools you will use to stay on it.

Be patient in getting to the goal setting. The foundation of your path, the interior journey, is crucial to navigating the outward expression of your faith.

Final Preparations

Imagine you are lacing up your hiking shoes to start walking your spiritual path. You know your *why* and have a good sense of *how* you are going to be moving on this pilgrimage. Your vision is to grow into the person God continually creates and calls you to be, given a desire to save your soul. Your path is yours uniquely. It is your responsibility to pace yourself on this journey. You will need to devote time and attention to this commitment. Leave your daily cares at the trailhead. You are not exactly sure where you will end up or what there is to see along the way. For now, your Spiritual Path plan in the back of the book is still blank, but whatever you choose to write on it will be sacred because it represents accepting an invitation to a life spent walking side by side with God.

Savor the journey!

Colloquy 2: How Do I Walk the Spiritual Path?

1. What emotions or insights are stirring inside me as I prepare for this journey of discerning a Spiritual Path plan? Remember that there are no right or wrong feelings; it is enough to simply acknowledge them.

2. Where am I most comfortable on the Cycle of Growth?

3. Where am I most likely to be challenged on the Cycle of Growth?

4. Is there any grace I need to walk this path?

My Walking Partner's response to what I have shared:

PART 2

BUEN CAMINO

Chapter 3

When Was I Moving toward God?

The Path of Consolation

Only in love can I find you, my God. In love the gates of my soul
spring open, allowing me to breathe a new air of freedom
and forget my own petty self.

KARL RAHNER, "GOD OF MY LIFE"

We start this journey with God from wherever we are in life at this moment. You can start walking your spiritual path at any day, hour, or moment. While God is present here and now next to you, within you, watching over you, within your community and relationships, often it is easier to see God's presence in hindsight. In hindsight,

- we are not so caught up in the emotions or busyness of the moment;
- we realize our worries and anxieties didn't come to fruition;
- we survived the unexpected; and
- we can sit as the observer of our own lives in gratitude for all that we were given.

In other words, hindsight is a gift.

The Ignatian *examen* prayer is the practice of finding God by reviewing each day in hindsight. Dennis Hamm, SJ, puts it into plain language with the title of his article "Rummaging for God: Praying Backwards through Your Day."[19] On the Spiritual Path, we look back over the previous year.

It seems the older a person gets, the faster each year goes. And yet so much changes in our lives in just six or twelve months. You are not the same person you were a year ago. But looking back much further than a year can lead to yearning for a different stage or life situation that is not an invitation to be where you are now. I absolutely loved being a fulltime mother, but I'm pretty sure that is not an invitation that is likely to come my way again, and I don't want to spend the time I have now wishing it would. A year is long enough to see the impact of the actions you took and yet short enough to remember the feelings or inner movements associated with those actions.

In Ignatian spirituality, the movement of a person's spirit toward God is called Consolation. It is not consolation in the sense of a consolation prize, as in, "Sorry, you didn't win," or in the sense of a funeral where we are seeking to be consoled. Consolation is described as a feeling of wholeness or unity with God. It is the sense you have that God is with you and you are reflecting that connection. Ignatius first recognized this spiritual consolation when he read *The Life of Christ* by Rudolph the Carthusian and books about the saints. Reading these books left him with a sense of joy. Eventually, reading those books led to a passionate desire to serve God by serving others. Consolation may be found in fleeting moments or in entire seasons of life. Like the kingdom of God, there are many ways to describe consolation, but none will do it total justice because language falls miserably short for encompassing an experience of movement toward God. Ignatius describes consolation as "every increase of hope, faith and charity, and all interior joy which calls and attracts to heavenly things."[20] *Ineffable* is the word that comes to mind for me. One fellow pilgrim described consolation as the John Denver song "You Fill Up My Senses." Sometimes consolation can cause physical reactions, such as chills or tingles, eyes welling with tears, and lumps in the throat. We all have consolations throughout our lives, even if we haven't specifically identified them as such.

It is very important to be aware of the fruit of consolation. Consolation brings energy and an awareness of others' needs and of the big picture beyond us and our fears. Consolation bonds us more closely to others and the world around us.

When I first had to write a letter to join the Ignatian Associates explaining why I wanted to do the Spiritual Exercises and join this faith community, all I could articulate in my letter was *yes!* I had no idea what would be asked of me or where this journey would take me or even who else would be on this journey with me other than my husband. But I knew enough to know the *yes!* that was in my heart. It was the same *yes!* when my husband asked me to marry him. The same *yes!* when I learned I was pregnant with my children. And the same *yes!* when I received Jinny Ditzler's blessing to write this book based on the structure of her goal-setting process. Those were big moments of consolation for me. Each was a response to an invitation to love more deeply and through new relationships.

Consolation doesn't come just in big, life-changing moments. Consolation can come in the ordinary moments of life when we recognize that the gift of love and connection to the Spirit of God is present. The moment of picking up my kids from school every day was a huge consolation for me. Walking in the door after work to a delicious smell is consolation for me not just because it is comforting but because I recognize the instant peace it brings and, in reflection, the connection to the bonds of love within the house. Every time my husband makes me laugh there is consolation. A moment of consolation can be fun and happy, but it can also bring a sense of wholeness, gratitude, relief, rightness, safety, and contentment. All of these conditions of life can reinforce a connection to the divine.

But consolation need not be associated only with the joyful moments of your life. There are moments of consolation that can be very hard, but you know in facing them and responding with love rather than hate or a myriad of ego defenses, that you are still moving closer to God. When you have to say to a parent who is dying, "It's okay to go. I love you," that's consolation. When you stay up all night with your sick child, forsaking your need for sleep because you want them to know they aren't alone, that is consolation. Often consolation can be twinged with desolation as well, a sense of bittersweetness because movement toward God can break the human heart. When you fight for justice and feel as if you are being overwhelmed by the powers working against you but you fight anyway, knowing it is the right thing to do, that is consolation. That is moving toward God. Consolation is recognizing those times when you experienced a sense of confidence in your judgment or actions, knowing you did the right thing or used your gifts wisely.

How to Discern Consolation

How do you know if something is a moment of consolation and moving toward God? Ignatius, through his own experience of trying to move toward God, identified very clear rules for the discernment of Spirits. Libraries of books along with the *Spiritual Exercises* have been written to share and teach these rules for discernment. The rules for discernment are not easy because often we want to think we are doing the will of God, when really we are only claiming something we want (or what the culture and society around us tell us to want) is God's will in order to justify our unhealthy actions. Spiritual directors go to school for years to recognize the movement of the Spirit toward and away from God in others, and even they are challenged to recognize these movements in themselves without the help of peers to hold them accountable.

Michael Buckley, SJ, offered a very clear understanding of consolation, lest we just look for all the good times when we were happy. He notes that consolation requires at least two characteristics: first, a desire from within that is positive—this feels good, right, holy, honorable, just, what God would want of me or be inviting me to; and second, the outcome, the long-term direction of this action is ultimately for goodness and the will of God. It is ultimately an act that may lead to love manifested as willing the good of another. At a moment of consolation, you will not likely know what the outcome or long-term implications are, but the orientation toward or away from God is likely clear. Both of those characteristics together—the desire of the heart and the long-term implication—point toward consolation and a movement toward God.

Consolation is not just what makes you happy but also what makes you whole. An emergency-room doctor who treats patients during a natural disaster is using her gifts in service to others. Some may not live, but in using her gifts, she is doing God's will and can be consoled that she was there and did whatever was possible to ease pain and suffering. Taking time away to retreat and recharge and take care of ourselves is a crucial means to consolation as well. Jesus modeled this self-care multiple times in the Gospels. However, there is a difference between going away from daily responsibilities to retreat and recharge and binging for forty-eight hours on alcohol until you pass out. I once had a fellow pilgrim excitedly ask, "So you are telling me it is the will of God that I go golfing for eight hours every weekend?" Well, not so fast. If golfing really gives you inner joy, that is one aspect of consolation (note the difference between inner joy and just having a good time or being entertained!). But what is the ultimate impact or desired outcome derived from eight hours of golf every weekend? Is your marriage stronger? Are you a better person? Are others served in some way? Are you glorifying God, that is, reflecting the person you are gifted to be, by golfing? Inner joy comes from recognizing the presence of God in any given moment. Those times of golfing may have indeed been consoling because they were moments of joy shared with others or times your soul found peace from being outside. Thus, there is a lesson to learn in those moments of consolation, but not necessarily a calling to make golf your life's focus. In the movie *Chariots of Fire*, Scottish Olympic athlete Eric Liddell feels called to be a runner. He says, "I believe that God made me for a purpose. But he also made me fast, and when I run, I feel his pleasure." *That* is consolation.

Here We Grow

While this first question on the Spiritual Path entails looking back on your past year, in terms of the Cycle of Growth, this question begins the See phase. You are seeing what consolations you experienced in the previous year. You need not judge them or question them. Don't doubt what comes to mind. Expect in faith that God is speaking to your heart. Don't do all the talking yourself. Listen for the memories that your Walking Partner wants to point out to you. "Look! Did you see us there?" Where would your Walking Partner say, "Did you feel our collaboration in that?" Start with your gut reaction to the question. The most powerful consolations usually jump to mind without prompting. Your heart knows them. Month by month, season by season, event by event, memory by memory. Only after some personal reflection and writing what comes to mind, use your calendar or any diary or journal you kept to remind yourself of all that you experienced. One fellow pilgrim went back through the pictures on her phone as a way to jog her memory. Allow yourself the freedom to just see where God was clearly present to you, with you, and through you in the past year.

Take as long as you like for this little stroll down memory lane. Once you have noted the obvious moments of consolation, these questions may help you see a few more. For example:

- Did you honestly do something to the best of your ability, giving it your all? Regardless of the outcome, did you feel fulfilled in the doing?
- Did you have an experience of Oneness in nature? In a relationship? In an activity or event?
- When did your heart leap at a revelation?
- When did you feel a deep sense of peace?
- Even in something that was really hard to do, did you walk away knowing you had done the right thing?
- Have you done something kind for a friend?
- In what ways did you take good care of your family or friends? In what ways were you taken care of?
- Were there times God sustained you, maybe through the capacities of others or prayer? What things did you do that affirmed your expression of faith?
- What activity led to your growth in some way? Did you learn new skills or develop your capacities that helped you grow? Were you able to put a problem behind you or make progress in the right direction?
- Where in the previous year were you using all your gifts and talents to serve others and to manifest the Spirit of God in this world?

There are no wrong answers here—write your list freely. This is your private list of the good stuff. Again, as a colloquy, imagine you are sharing these moments in conversation with your Walking Partner. Listen for what your Walking Partner has to say as well. You will probably be pleasantly surprised—most people are. Tears of joy are welcomed!

Colloquy 3: My Moments of Consolation

Where in the past year was I moving closer to God and being the person my heart desires to be?

My Walking Partner's response to what I have shared:

By looking back, we recognize the good that we often missed because we were too caught up in the worries of the moment. Can you recognize in this survey of your past year that the vast majority of things you worried about didn't happen? Were you able to prevent them by some action you did, or were they fears that were just taking you away from the goodness of the moment at hand? Far too often we focus on the bad things that have happened or on our worries about the future. We let those negative spirits take root in our mindset instead of focusing on the good that we were able to pull off in the face of all the challenges around us. Not only does this focus on finding the goodness in our lives remind us that there is goodness to come down the road, but it also gives us the lightness of gratitude to move forward rather than the weight of worry to hold us back.

Reading through this list with another person, such as a spiritual director or friend who is doing their own Spiritual Path plan, is a beautiful way to honor and animate your moments of consolation. How quick we are to share with others our to-do list; how rarely we share our where-I-experienced-God list. These are times you felt in collaboration with your Walking Partner. That is a huge gift for someone else to hear.

Finally, share a note of gratitude with your Walking Partner for all of these moments. Ideally, you will look for these moments daily, becoming ever more mindful of their presence within it to keep you going in the tough spots. Ignatius instructs us to use these moments to build fortitude for the desolate days to come. Be humble, and recognize that these moments are not of our orchestration. They are gifts from God. Be aware that God is with you now. That inner joy is possible. And that you have what it takes to experience and collaborate with God in the coming months.

Chapter 4

When Was I Moving away from God?

The Path of Desolation

Jesus said to him, "If you wish to be perfect, go, sell your possessions, and give the money to the poor, and you will have treasure in heaven; then come, follow me." When the young man heard this word, he went away grieving, for he had many possessions.

MATTHEW 19:21–22

Although the loving Spirit is always present, sometimes we lose our connection with it. There is just too much muck! Sometimes, that muck is truly on us, and sometimes it comes from beyond us, but still, it can block our path. Before we can set a healthy plan for our future, we need to acknowledge the desolations of our past.

St. Ignatius writes, "Desolation is darkness or disturbance of the soul, movement to low and earthly things, disquiet from various agitations and temptations, moving to lack of confidence, without hope, without love, finding oneself totally slothful, tepid, sad and as if separated from one's Creator and Lord."[21] God is not absent during these times, but it can definitely feel that way. Doubts, temptations, self-preoccupations, restlessness, and feeling cut off from others are all hallmarks of desolation. Such feelings, in Ignatius's words, "move one toward lack of faith and leave one without hope and without love."[22]

Richard Rohr, OFM, distinguishes between two paths of darkness. One is the desolation we choose by ignoring the call of the Spirit or by separating ourselves from God, "by being selfish (living out of the false or separate self)" or what he just calls "stupidity."[23] These are times we humans do dumb, stupid, rude, or thoughtless things because we aren't seeing the world around us as permeated with the presence of God. Instead, we act in ways that protect our ego, defend our pride, and lash out. The second path is the path of darkness that, through little or no fault of our own, desolation washes over us. This is the time of tragedy in life, the moments we feel abandoned, or when others inappropriately lash out at us out of their woundedness. These are the times of experiencing the natural human survival instincts of fight, flight, freeze, flop, friend, or fawn trauma reaction.[24] These are not times of choosing to move away from God but rather times when we just can't connect with the presence of God that is all around us. These are the Holy Saturdays of our lives that often last seasons or years. We can sit for a painfully long time in desolation until we learn whatever it is that must be learned.

My Journey

It was eight o'clock on a Wednesday night, my sixteenth day in the hospital without a diagnosis, when my doctor came in and confirmed I had a very rare stage 4 lymphoma and a fifty-fifty chance of survival at one year. Three weeks earlier I had been venturing around Seattle with my college-age daughter with no hint of any illness. The desolation was almost instantaneous. I went numb. Life was instantly surreal. Even with years of prayer, meditation, reflection, and faith practice in my experience, I felt God was nowhere to be found in that moment or in many moments of shock to come. The ache of my soul in having to face leaving my husband and children was torturous. I have no doubt God was more present to me that night than during any other night in my life, and yet it wasn't humanly possible to experience that Infinite Love in the state I was in. I was desolate.

Everybody has times of desolation. God is in those times too, not causing them, but in them, with us, within us. Again, the rules for discernment of spirits are needed. The inner movement of our spirit as well as the ultimate orientation must be considered to see if what is happening is an invitation for faithfulness and growth or a temptation to move away from God. Sin is the illusion of separation from God. It is our choice not to trust in the divine Presence. With

God's grace, we work ourselves out of sin, that illusion of separateness, through brutal self-honesty, confession, surrender, forgiveness, apology, and restitution.

Consolation and desolation are first and foremost about interior movements. While, on the outside, an experience may appear to be a great achievement, it can easily be symptomatic of an interior desolation. Many people who have achieved great things have done so at the cost of their souls. Along the way to success, they failed to take care of themselves or those around them or to maintain their ethics, or they harmed the human dignity of others in the process. They may have achieved their goal, but they did not move closer to God in the process.

A note about desolation brought on by others. Several different people have been quoted as saying, "Resentment is like taking a poison pill and hoping the other person dies." Truly the actions of others are a source of angst in our hearts. But allowing their actions, however painful and egregious, to draw us away from our growth toward God is ultimately our choice. Often, we nurse resentment long after the action that caused it is gone. Thomas Aquinas defines love as "willing the good of another." What is truly good for another person may be for them to see the error of their ways, to come to justice, to repent for the times they have hurt us. But this is a different desire. It is a desire for their wholeness rather than our desire for revenge or a wish to see them suffer. When it comes to the pain others have caused us, are we able to move toward God ourselves and will what is good for them, or are we moving away from God and nursing the resentment that is slowly only killing our own soul?

Empty rituals can also be a source of desolation. Having a huge ceremony to celebrate a wedding may indeed be a moment of consolation when both parties feel called to the sacrament and the long-term direction is for a lifelong loving commitment. However, a wedding celebration of a child marriage or when one person is feeling compelled by some outside entity to participate is not a moment of consolation. That marriage, even if performed in a church with all the proper rituals, is not celebrating growth toward God. No empty ritual can propel us toward God. This includes church services and fulfilling habitual obligations without any inner joy from participation in community life.

For years in consulting with faith-based organizations and individuals, I struggled with the lack of true spiritual integration in the process or goals set. As I reflected on the movement of the Spirit within me, that desolation or annoyance kept coming up. One thing I have learned through Ignatian spirituality: when we experience prolonged uneasiness about something, it generally means we are being invited to do something about it. Ultimately, I had to choose to stop doing what felt desolating or to adapt it to integrate a healthy sense of spirituality. The result is this book, but it wouldn't have happened without my noticing the desolation I was experiencing.

Unfortunately, humans have an even easier time lying to themselves than they do to each other. We come up with justifications to deny the angst in our hearts. Sometimes there is angst to do the right thing, but we reason it is just too hard or too countercultural, and we let fear inhibit us. And sometimes we feel angst because we know we are moving away from God, but we justify doing so with cultural norms, or the immediate gratification of an action blinds us to the long-term implications for our souls. We consume more than we really need when we are called to live simply. We procrastinate, deny, or substitute harmful substances and behaviors instead of taking an honest look in the mirror and admitting we need God's help to overcome our insecurities. We harm those we love the most as well as total strangers, reasoning they are in the wrong or bad or deserving of our scorn rather than admitting we might be in need of the growth God offers us to be in healthy relationship with them.

Unhealthy Spiritualities around Desolation

Going through my cancer journey, I have heard many unhealthy spiritualities around desolation. I know people often don't know what to say and they still want to give me hope, but the future is truly unknown. In Ignatian spirituality, God is Infinite Love, not infinite control. As you reflect on the desolations of the past year, recognize if you are adding to the desolation by blaming or attributing it to your Walking Partner in one of these ways.

1. "This desolation is a punishment from God." *No!* Just like in the return of the Prodigal Son, God doesn't punish. God celebrates our return to wholeness. The Hebrew Scriptures speak of God punishing people, but the deeper lesson is always a natural consequence for not following the law of love and faith.

2. "This is a test from God." *No!* Even Ignatius noted this possible explanation for desolation, but in translation it can also be said to be an invitation to growth. I have found many blessings in my cancer journey and have grown through desolate times. Sometimes the hardest experiences are exactly what we need to get over ourselves, but that doesn't mean God was testing me. Rather, I think, through the darkest hours God was holding me.

3. "God has a plan." *No!* This unhealthy spirituality again makes God a puppeteer of our lives. God's plan is to work through us in a boundless relationship of love to build the kingdom of God, a world of love, creativity, and mercy for everyone. The steps of that plan are the invitations of our lives. God's plan was not that I get cancer. That came from bodily functions not working as expected. God didn't plan for World War II or any violent acts—all of those were choices by humans. God doesn't send tornadoes to destroy towns; rather, cold fronts and warm fronts collide and naturally produce high winds. God's plan is that when these desolations happen, God can be found in the consolation of people coming together to support one another.

4. "God never gives you more than you can carry." *No!* God does not give suffering. Rather, suffering comes from choices not to love by ourselves or others. Sometimes our desolations are more than we can carry, especially alone. People do have mental and spiritual breakdowns. We are limited creatures. But we only add to the burdens of others when we imply they aren't strong enough to carry something.

5. "Others have it worse." *No!* There is no comparative suffering or joy. I have a friend who is both legally deaf and blind. During my cancer journey she would fret that my hardships were so much worse than hers. I don't think I would last a day in her situation, but trying to get my head around her suffering just added to my own. We each walk our own path and find our own significance and connection to God in our experience.

As you can see from the examples discussed above, unhealthy spiritualities around desolation ingratiate themselves into real-life situations with many different expressions, and in many different disguises. Spend some time thinking about unhealthy spiritualities that may be lurking in your heart.

Where Is God in Your Desolation?

For some people, naming the moments of desolation over the past year feels a bit like making a confession or going to reconciliation. There is angst about admitting where we have diminished ourselves, let alone what we have done to others. The reluctance to reflect on desolation is definitely a temptation to avoid that growth. But trust the process. Have confidence in the plan. Start by determining: Where is God within this desolation?

Perhaps God is in the invitation, the desire you have, to leave it behind and be healed of it. Remember, you are not in desolation now. You are doing this process to move closer to God. By intentionally walking this Spiritual Path to move toward God you are able to stand outside the moments of desolation you have experienced and observe them from the safety of this time and with your Walking Partner. You may have felt alone then, but you are not now. Admitting to yourself the downside of the previous year frees you to move beyond it. Often when we name something that is weighing on us, that is half the battle, and we can then let it go. There is no need to get caught up in that desolation again when walking this part of your spiritual path. We can face these desolations knowing we are infinitely loved, even when we can't feel it, when we screw up, when we fall short, when we are in darkness.

My Journey

I came to understand this lesson when I was literally facing death. My doctors gave me twenty-four hours to decide to undergo a transplant that, at best, would buy me a few more months to maybe a year. Meanwhile, the ordeal would be exhaustive to my 24–7 caregivers. It would mean putting my body through chemo, radiation, pills, and bone marrow biopsies. It would entail continuing on an emotional roller-coaster and potentially depleting us financially. The alternative was to call hospice and accept that I had about three weeks to live.

My spiritual director told me there were no right or wrong answers. Neither was there a plan that I had to figure out in twenty-four hours. The only thing important for me to know was that God loved me at this moment, and that I would be loved at the moment of my death *or* at every moment of treatment—and that this Love was bigger and more powerful than anything, including death.

You are in the See phase of the Cycle of Growth. You aren't in the Judge phase of the cycle, so this is not a time for punishing yourself or someone else for the darkness you experienced. No blame. Just name the reality as you experienced it. Observe the big picture with the clarity of some hindsight but without getting caught up in the emotional cesspool. This is not only Ignatian but also Psych 101: we can't reframe or learn from something unless we name it first.

In the same way, what initially may appear to be the darkest hour may actually be the catalyst for glorifying God beyond anything your imagination could fathom. God is there with you in that darkness and turmoil, calling you to recognize the way out perhaps, so that in time you can lead others out too. In *The Dark Night of the Soul*, St. John of the Cross detailed his long period of desolation and angst. He writes of the emptiness and horror his soul went through, "a purgation," before it could experience divine Love. Ignatius, too, went through months of desolation during which he condemned himself for the person he once was. Bill Wilson, founder of Alcoholics Anonymous, wrote most of the Twelve-Step process in total despair. In his desolation he wrote about the death of all ego that was required in order for God to free him from his addiction. In detailing his journey, he helped countless others do so as well.

Seeing the Desolations of the Past Year

Start by seeking two very closely tied spiritual graces: gentleness and honesty. My spiritual director's words, *Be gentle with yourself, and be truly honest with yourself,* reverberate constantly in my head. These desolations you are naming do not define you. You are a child of God, infinitely and unconditionally loved. It is safe and healthy for you to admit those things that have been barriers keeping you from connecting to that Infinite Love and mercy. Hear God's voice saying, "Neither do I condemn you" (John 8:11). For now, don't worry about sharing these desolations with anyone else. No one else needs to see them, but you need to articulate them. You need to be free of them.

For some people, naming the desolations of the past year can be done in twenty minutes of prayerful reflection. For others, admitting desolations takes longer and might entail some professional counseling. Similar to recalling moments of consolation, there will be some desolations that are eager to jump out and be named. Allow yourself time and space for your times of desolation to be revealed to you. One of the most significant and painful desolations of my life came to me four days after a moment when I had disregarded someone else who was in desperate need. I was sitting in my kitchen making breakfast when it hit me how, hiding behind fabricated justifications, I had truly ignored a clear invitation to care for someone else. I burst into tears right then and there.

Consider the following questions as you and your Walking Partner once again walk down memory lane of the previous year:

- Were there times you let yourself or others down or they let you down?
- Did you experience physical or mental challenges that affected you?
- What setbacks at work or in your family life were painful?
- Did you miss opportunities that still haunt you?
- Did you experience relationships that floundered?
- Can you admit times where you let your high standards lapse?
- What led to gaps in your experiences of joy and sense of wholeness?
- Were there times you resisted opportunities for growth?
- Did you feed resentments rather than will the good for your enemies?
- Did you struggle through empty ritual or relationships?

Prayer for Walking the Path of Desolation
Dear Lord,
Help me to see those moments of desolation in my life
over the past year.
Help me to be gentle with myself and not use these moments
to belittle myself as your co-laborer.
Help me to be honest with you and myself.
Help me to be free of the burden of carrying them.
Help me to name them so they no longer have a hold on me.
Help me to know they do not define me.

Colloquy 4: My Moments of Desolation

When in the past year was I moving away from God and not being the person my heart desires to be?

My Walking Partner's response to what I have shared:

In the *Spiritual Exercises*, Ignatius advises us to never make a decision in a time of desolation but instead to wait it out with patience, trusting that God is with you and that consolation will return one day.

When you are confident that you have identified your most challenging moments of desolation from the past year, sit back and breathe. You are safe. In fact, you are now just a little bit stronger. Growth is never easy, and what you just did was something not everyone is willing to do. Hopefully you feel some consolation in having named those desolations. You have taken an important step down your spiritual path.

Sharing Your Desolations

Verbally sharing desolations is at the heart of therapy, reconciliation, and recovery. When you sit with a trusted person such as a spiritual director, fellow pilgrim, spouse, or friend and read this list of desolations, you grow stronger. Darkness hates the light. I have found at Spiritual Path retreats that the best person to hear your desolations can be a stranger who you will likely never see again. Verbally articulating desolations breaks the cycle that keeps them spinning in our heads and puts them on the table so that we *control* them instead of *reacting* to their influence. Speaking desolations doesn't make them go away, but it does loosen their grip on our hearts.

Listening to another person sharing their desolations is not the time to lessen the pain of desolation or one-up their pain by saying something like, "Oh, you think that's bad? One time I . . . (insert your story of pain)." The best response is gratitude for their courage in sharing something so painful and personal, and compassion for the burden they have carried inside. In your own words it is always safe to say, "I'm so sorry you had to go through that. Thank you for having the courage to share it with me."

Moving Forward on the Spiritual Path

These first two questions of the Spiritual Path, reviewing your consolations and desolations, are both in the See phase of the Cycle of Growth. Your observations of where you have moved toward and away from God in the past year are setting the stage for moving into the Judge phase in the next question, which is, *What is God inviting me to learn?*

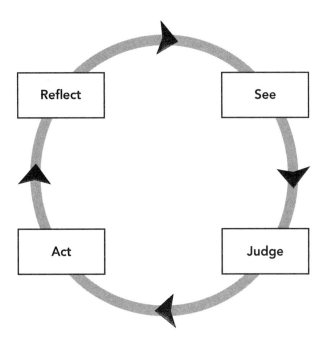

Chapter 5

What Is God Inviting Me to Learn?

Signposts on Your Spiritual Path

When we are lost in the woods,
the sight of a signpost is a great matter.

C. S. LEWIS

The jaunt down the path of consolation and the path of desolation from the previous year served three purposes. First, you now have a sense of how God is present throughout your life and how those inner senses of joy and angst are strong indicators of that Presence. Becoming more attuned to those inner movements of the heart and recognizing what they are trying to tell you is what Ignatian spirituality is all about. Did you happen to notice that many of those times of consolation and desolation were not in what we would traditionally consider prayer times? God is with us throughout our days, as readily present as the air we breathe.

Second, these colloquies are good practice for prayer because they are real experiences you have had, not just conversations with your Walking Partner about hopes, dreams, anxieties, or petitions. You know what was stirring inside you during them. We can share most fully and honestly from experience.

Beyond recognizing God's presence in the past year and getting comfortable being honest with your Walking Partner, naming your consolations and desolations provides the seeds for the lessons God is inviting you to learn as you start to walk this Spiritual Path. Every season of life holds new lessons to be learned. It may take you a whole year to learn them, to fully digest them into your *modus operandi*, but here is where you start. These lessons are not the goals to be reached but the habits you need to develop to make progress on your spiritual path. These lessons will guide you more in *how* you are walking rather than *where* you are heading. There is great value in learning from our moments of consolation and desolation from the past year. The dark times are spaces of growth, and the light times cheer us on.

Lessons to Be Learned from the Past

You are moving from the See phase of the growth cycle to the Judge phase by identifying lessons to be learned. This is the topic of your next colloquy with your Walking Partner. Talk about what in those lists speaks to you and, as with any conversation, pause to listen after you have shared what's on your mind. In the Judge phase, we consider and chat about our consolations and desolations in light of the Gospels. What stories come to mind as related to your experience? Where did Christ or the apostles go through something similar, and how did they respond?

This exercise is similar to when Ignatius realized that his fantasies of medieval courtly glory left him feeling empty, whereas his dreams of saintly actions in the service of God left him feeling excited and hopeful for his future. Writing in the third person, St. Ignatius said of himself, "But he paid no attention to this, nor did he stop to weigh the difference until one day his eyes were opened a little and he began to wonder at the difference and to reflect on it, learning from experience that one kind of thoughts left him sad and the other cheerful."[25] This analysis was the seed for his conversion to a life dedicated to God. So too is this your opportunity to have your eyes opened to the lessons God invites you to learn from your experiences of consolation and desolation.

To identify the lessons to be learned, review both the consolations and desolations much like an analyst or detached observer might do. Don't get caught up in either the inner joy or the inner angst at this stage. Instead, look back and identify what made those moments possible and what was their impact. This allows you to learn how to set the stage for having more moments of consolation down the road. Name them. Remember, this is not about punishing yourself for anything you did or didn't do. Detach your emotions here. While reviewing your desolations, pay particular attention to your motivations.

Don't shy away from noting any lessons. You are not committing to them here; you are simply articulating what you see, as well as the patterns of behavior as they are related to your consolations and desolations. Look for patterns across your experiences, especially for those consolations or desolations that have happened multiple times. Write down whatever thoughts occur to you. Just name what you observe. You don't need to specify a lesson for every consolation and desolation, but you should identify at least five to seven lessons that would make a difference in your life.

Here are some examples from past Spiritual Path retreats.

Consolation/Desolation	Lesson I Am Being Invited to Learn
• Coming back to my home at the end of most days felt calming.	• Keep home time and environment a priority.
• I didn't take any vacation.	• I need more balance in my life.
• Being with the kids was so great!	• I really enjoy being a part of my children's lives.
• I didn't reach an important work goal.	• I need more support to get where I want to be.

The following questions might help you identify the lessons God invites you to learn from your consolations and desolations.

Don't forget to listen for your Walking Partner's response.

Lessons from Consolations

- What about that moment gave me consolation?
- When I did something that really gave me joy, was it the action I really enjoyed, the person for whom I did the action, or the setting of the action? How was I different at that time compared to other times when I didn't notice such consolation?
- How did my consolation lead me toward God? What made me so open to that moment/time? How do I get more of that?

Lessons from Desolations

- What could I have done to better engage God in this?
- How did that desolation lead me away from God?
- What fear or greater concern was driving me?
- Were there ways I reacted in those moments that made things worse?
- Are there things I could do to avoid being in that situation again, knowing the same desolation is likely to recur?
- What wisdom is God trying to share with me about me?

Colloquy 5: Lessons I Am Being Invited to Learn

My Walking Partner's response to what I have shared:

You have likely come up with many lessons you could take to heart. Again, no punishing yourself here. This is a brainstorming analysis of your previous year and how to get more of the good stuff and less of the empty stuff. Read through the list of lessons as if you were reading it back to your Walking Partner. Your Walking Partner is your best life coach. Does your Walking Partner have any other lessons to add?

Judge: Which Signposts Do I Really Need to Follow?

In this next colloquy, discern with your Walking Partner which three lessons you need to truly embrace to stay moving toward the co-laborer you are called to be. Yes, just three. You will return to these lessons each month to acknowledge how well you heeded them and the impact of doing so. For now, write each lesson you choose on line *a*.

Colloquy 6: Judge Three Lessons I am Being Invited to Learn (line *a*)

Colloquy 7: Turning Lessons into Signposts (line *b*)

1. a.

   b.

2. a.

   b.

3. a.

   b.

Notice that these lessons aren't blatantly spiritual. You can have lessons that advise you to "Pray before each meeting" or "Go to church every week" if those reflect the patterns and habits you feel you need to learn. However, a person who prays for an hour a day but then habitually works overtime to the detriment of the family has not learned how to set themselves up for consolation. We are seeking to recognize God teaching us throughout our lives, not just in religious spaces or practices. When you walk a Spiritual Path regularly, you realize there is a spirituality in all that you do, even those seemingly practical or logistical habits you keep, because you are being invited by God to learn from them. These lessons are for you to make your spiritual journey smoother, wherever you may end up.

Reading the Signs

Now, turn your lessons into Signposts that will help guide you on your Spiritual Path. Signposts are like the repetitive signs you see on the freeway, reminding you of the healthy and safe way to drive (e.g., Buckle Up for Safety. Speed limit 55. Caution when Flashing). They aren't telling you where to go but how to get where you are going safely. That is what these Signposts are for you: how to build on the knowledge of the past. Your Signposts can be new skills or abilities or habits or major life lessons. They are rules, reminders, or advice for yourself. I like to make my Signposts sound more like orders than like mere suggestions. After I recognized a pattern of hiding behind threads of e-mails, my Signpost read "Pick up the damn phone!" After I noticed a pattern of missing commitments, my Signpost shouted, "GET IT ON THE CALENDAR NOW!"

Signposts vary for all stages of life.

Here are some examples of life lessons turned into Signposts.

Life Lesson	Signpost for My Spiritual Path
• Volunteering for extra projects made me feel that I contributed something.	• Raise your hand!
• Keep home time and environment a priority.	• Jump on grandma's feather bed!
• I need more friends and community.	• Connect through real conversations!

• I really enjoy being a part of my children's lives.	• Make way for Kid Time!
• I need more support to get where I want to be.	• Call in the reinforcements!

Here are some other Signposts that fellow pilgrims have committed to and wanted to share. Each came from looking back over a year and recognizing the need to learn this lesson to set themselves up for more consolation.

Be present to people! Enjoy them!
Feel the wind in your hair!
Run a little every day.
Hand over outcomes (to God).

Each Signpost has the following parameters:

- **Positive!** What *to* do rather than what *not* to do.
- **Memorable.** Use wording that expresses the meaning exactly. (Maybe use an inside joke or hidden meaning only you know.)
- **Short.** This is not a parental lecture but a motivational logo! Five words is a good maximum.
- **Start with a verb.** You are going to act upon these lessons, not just think about them.

Take a few minutes now to go back and rewrite those lessons as Signposts for your Spiritual Path on line *b* of the previous colloquy using the parameters noted above. Continue to be aware of what moves inside of you as you find the wording that seems just right.

Your Signposts will be with you for the life of this Spiritual Path plan. Ideally, that is for the next year or six months, but not for the rest of your life, because in time, you will naturally incorporate them into your way of being. Once you have spent a year continually practicing these habits, they will be your way of proceeding. You can then move on to identify new Signpost reminders for your next plan.

Make sure each of your three Signposts is powerful and memorable to you. Read them out loud. Imagine how they would look printed on a signpost that you walk by every so often on your path. One of my fellow pilgrims said to me, "Signpost? I need these to be a flashing neon billboard!"

Act!

This is an exciting moment. Finally, you are beginning to draft your Spiritual Path. In our mini Cycle of Growth, this is where you act. You are committing to embracing the advice on these three Signposts. These are the lessons that you and your Walking Partner discerned together out of everything that happened in your life in the previous year. Every month as you revisit your Spiritual Path, you will assess how well you have heeded this advice and what difference it has made to your journey. In writing your Signposts on your Spiritual Path plan you can breathe a sigh of gratitude and relief that your past is now behind you. You have recognized what God invited you to learn. It is time to close that chapter, knowing you have honored it, listened to it, and grown from it.

Turn to the back of the book to the blank My Spiritual Path page, and write your three Signposts on the space allotted on your plan as if you are writing your own Scripture.

Reflect. The Scenic Overlook

You have already reached the first scenic overlook of your Spiritual Path journey. Your calling for this journey is to discern a plan to put your faith into action. Recall that the ultimate horizon of the Spiritual Path is the Principle and Foundation: to praise, reverence, and serve God by being the person I am called to be, the person I am capable of being in my given time and context, and in so doing to save my soul. You are a co-laborer with God in this glorious lifetime.

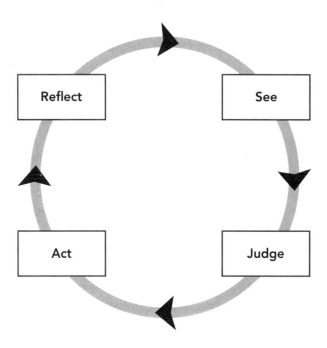

You looked back over the past year and saw the moments of consolation, movement toward God, and of desolation, movement away from God. As you moved into the Judge phase, you identified lessons God was inviting you to learn. You turned those lessons into Signposts and judged which three would make the most significant impact on your journey in the coming year. Then you acted by adding those Signposts to your Spiritual Path with a commitment to practice them. Now is the time to reflect on how completing this process felt. What moved inside you as you went through each phase of the cycle? Did anything surprise you along the way? What difference did your Walking Partner make? At the end of this process, do you feel gratitude? Resistance? Energy? There are no right or wrong feelings. Acknowledge your efforts and celebrate what you learned. Whatever you are feeling, you have grown just a bit since you started walking.

Colloquy 8: Reflections from the First Leg of the Journey

What did I experience by taking these first steps on my Spiritual Path and articulating my Signposts?

My Walking Partner's response:

On a real hike, this would be the point where you would have worked the kinks out of your muscles and would have established a comfortable stride. You are gaining confidence that this was a good trail to take today. Remember to pace yourself for the long trail ahead. Now that the Signposts are in place, this next leg of the journey is designed to help you create a faithful internal compass.

Chapter 6

How Do I Confront the Spirit *Not* of God?

Claiming Your Sacred Mantra

"You are braver than you believe, stronger than you seem,
and smarter than you think."

A. A. MILNE

"And more loved than you can imagine."

LISA KELLY

The fourth question on your Spiritual Path is the most challenging, but it promises to make the biggest difference to your experience over the next several months. This part of the journey gets at the heart of the spiritual life for every person: claiming your identity.

Meeting the Spirit *Not* of God

Saint Ignatius came from a military background. After his conversion he continued to see his devotion to God in terms of military imagery. Essentially, he became a warrior for Christ, devoted to love and compassion and all that Christ represented. But every warrior must have an enemy. As a follower of Christ, he was called to love all people, so who then was his adversary? During his time convalescing and later in Manresa when he was writing the *Spiritual Exercises*, it became increasingly clear to him that his greatest adversary to his relationship with God was within himself. Think about that revelation for a moment. Imagine that your greatest adversary is within yourself! There may be people who blatantly call you names or harm you. There may be diseases or systems working against your desires. There may be a culture around you that in no way reflects your values, so you are constantly struggling against it. But none of these are under your control. The people, systems, and cultures that disrupt your path to wholeness and fulfillment are what you need to honestly face. You recognize that you control only yourself, your response, and how much of your power you choose to give these barriers. The greatest adversary to collaborating with God is within yourself.

Ignatius realized the importance of discerning the movement of the spirits within his heart. He also came to recognize a spirit *not* of God at work within himself. This spirit *not* of God tempted him with moments of false consolation and deep desolation that actually led him away from the will of God. This spirit *not* of God is formidable with its own temptations and unhealthy desires to get us to do anything but praise and glorify God by being our full selves. The Gospels tell us that Jesus himself experienced the spirit *not* of God in the desert with temptations of security, power, and prestige. If the deepest desire of the Spirit of God is for us to be fully who we are created to be and thus reflect the glory of God in our unique being, the deepest desire of the spirit *not* of God is for people to be less than what God created them to be. This spirit wants us to become diminished beings, weaklings, empty shells that are never strong enough to reflect or enact the love of God.

For Ignatius, the human soul is an ongoing battlefield between the Spirit of God and the spirit *not* of God. We are free to choose which Spirit to follow and which messages to believe about ourselves. Are we beloved children of God called to fulfill the deepest healthy desires of our hearts? The desires God shares with us, for us? Or are we useless creatures who are both unlovable and incapable of loving others? Incapable of fulfilling our purpose in this life? The internal battle rages in both subtle and overt moments.

The world around us, including those people, systems, and cultures that hold us down, is the manifestation of people who have a battle for the fulfillment of their souls raging inside. But if you focus only on battling the spirit *not* of God within another person's soul, that spirit *not* of God is just frolicking away within your own. We all have our own work to do within ourselves first.

This idea of an active spirit *not* of God at work in this life can be as challenging for people to grasp as the concept of a Higher Power. Some may simply give credence to a devil or the power of evil. Some may see it as the manifestation of original sin. Some people accept that it is human nature to have a dark side. Some people may feel a negative energy at work, while others say this is nothing more than our desire to protect our egos. Some call it our innate woundedness. Alcoholics and addicts can be identified by brain scans that indicate parts of their brain to be functioning incorrectly. It is what the disease of addiction does to a body, and yet, even they will still refer to their disease as a demon and alcohol as "cunning, baffling, and powerful."[26] If it makes sense for you, personify this force that is working against you. However you conceive of the spirit *not* of God, it is the power that constantly seeks to lead you away from your spiritual path of growing closer to God and the person you were created to be.

In *The Screwtape Letters* by C. S. Lewis, a fictional devil mentors a younger demon in the ways of evil. One of the clearest lessons the devil tells his young mentee is to not let the subject believe that evil exists, for if they don't know evil exists, they can't fight against it. People will simply accept all the havoc evil wreaks as a normal part of life, beyond their control. In walking your Spiritual Path and seeking to move closer to God, you have a choice to admit there are forces at work against you in this endeavor, forces within you, within your own psyche and heart, that don't want you to recognize your full potential.

So often we think of the spirit *not* of God as causing only serious evil—war, murder—in the world. But the spirit *not* of God is much more subtle, needing only small habits or brief moments of resistance to lead us from our spiritual path. It is the collective of all those brief moments of resistance that lead to the wars and the murders and the more blatant evil that happens. Again, a good spiritual director can spot that spirit *not* of God at work within us a mile away, most notably in the statements we say about ourselves. My spiritual director is constantly catching me, "Did you just hear yourself?" There are no throw-away comments, no self-effacing tag lines allowed in this process. If you are walking this spiritual path, if you believe you were created to praise, reverence, and serve God and by that means fulfill your soul, turn off that inner voice of the spirit *not* of God that tries to deny your dignity and belittle your identity.

Ignatius's rules for discernment identify how this spirit *not* of God works through false consolations and desolations. The spirit *not* of God builds up those things that feel good but actually lead us away from the person we are called to be. Ignatius identifies things like honor, pride, and riches, and notes that the spirit *not* of God makes these things appear to be consolations that give our souls joy. For example, being offered a more prestigious position with a larger salary but work in a position that does not utilize your talents and actually leaves you desolate might be a serious temptation rather than a celebrated achievement. The spirit *not* of God can also put us into desolation and turn us away from our calling with false messages about ourselves that reinforce our perceived weaknesses. These are the voices in our heads and the messages we give ourselves to justify not being the person we are called to be when we stray from our spiritual path.

To confront that spirit *not* of God in your life requires several steps in this chapter. Through them we continue to work that Cycle of Growth, beginning with honestly seeing the reality of how we show up for daily life.

Naming Your Limiting Behaviors

To identify how you are allowing that spirit *not* of God to push you off your spiritual path, start by listing honestly all the *behaviors* you do that you would characterize as unhealthy, troublesome, or at least regrettable. What patterns of behavior do others sometimes call you out on? What are the things you *do* that lead to frustration with yourself or to outcomes you don't want? What do you do that leads to desolation or false consolations? In contrast to our previous questions about past *events* you learned from, here we are looking deeper into ongoing *behaviors*. What annoys you about you?

In the interest of transparency, here's part of one of my old lists:

- I waste time on the computer.
- I isolate myself.
- I don't pray consistently.
- I spin thoughts in my head.

- I lose my stuff all the time.
- I eat too many sweets.
- I don't speak up for myself.
- I have no discipline.

I could easily spit out about a dozen or so actual behaviors that are limiting me moving toward God. These are things I actually do. I am naming them, or *seeing* them. They are facts. I *do* these things. When I look back on my day and my actions, these are the things I wish I had done differently or the behaviors that somehow place a barrier between me and others. I am not condemning myself for them. I am still sitting in a safe space, and I am admitting them on this piece of paper. Something is telling me that at least some of these behaviors are limiting me from being the person I am called to be.

Begin by brainstorming whatever behaviors come to you quickly. Whatever you do, don't avoid writing something down because you don't want to deal with it. Write everything down and you can discern later, with help from your Walking Partner, what your next step will be. For now, just be willing to see, free of judgment, *the things that you do or don't do* that are limiting you.

Colloquy 9: Naming My Limiting Behaviors

My Walking Partner's response:

Listening to the Spirit *Not* of God: Your Limiting Voice

The experiences we have in our lives come from the behaviors or actions we do or don't do. Those include the behaviors you just listed. Those behaviors come from somewhere. We choose to do them. The reason for doing or not doing any behavior may be conscious or subconscious until we reflect upon it enough to bring it to light. Remember, the step before Act is Judge. Our judgments are based not only on factual information but also on our beliefs and assumptions shaped throughout our lives. They often make up the filter for what we see. These assumptions are the messages we constantly hear in our heads—a way of thinking about ourselves, someone else, or circumstances. Those voices and messages were largely formed in childhood as our personalities developed. They may be the messages we heard from our parents or influential teachers or friends, or they may have been our own responses to situations we encountered while having impressionable hearts, minds, and egos. Some of our voices empower us: "I can make a difference here." However, some are limiting voices: "No one likes me," or "The world is against me." How many times have you, often in a moment of desolation, broken down and said, "I am so . . ." (fill in the negative attribute: stupid, lazy, ugly, lame, unloved). We tell them to ourselves so often that we have come to believe they are the truth, fact, unchangeable. But what if they aren't true? What if those negative messages we secretly tell ourselves about who we are or about life in general, even subconsciously, are actually a dark spirit *not* of God at work?

They are just messages. They are not facts, and they are not truth. You have heard that life is a self-fulfilling prophecy. So which prophecy are you going to listen to? The one that says you are powerful beyond anything you can imagine because you have the Spirit of God working through you? Or the one that says you are powerless because you are so broken and undesirable, especially compared to everyone else?

Unfortunately, just as you have a unique calling as a collaborator with God, you also have a unique wound that the spirit *not* of God loves to exploit.

Remember, these are messages we give to ourselves about ourselves or our perspective. These messages could be said to come from the Spirit of God and the spirit *not* of God battling within us. Did you notice, even in listing your limiting behaviors, a twinge of desire in your heart for them not to be so? God is in that desire.

The Spirit of God offers us the gifts of growth, courage, patience, passion, wisdom, and so much more. God calls us to be everything we can be: a unique reflection of God's self. This is the voice that whispers, *I am loved. I am capable. I have important insights to share.* The spirit *not* of God seeks to limit that growth with a voice that diminishes us. All too often we make that limiting voice our own without realizing it. We come to believe things like *I am unlovable. I am so stupid. I will never be satisfied. I have nothing to contribute.* This is where it is most vital to have that healthy understanding of God in your mind. A God of Infinite Love never diminishes a person.

Here is the connection between that list of behaviors you wrote and recognizing the spirit *not* of God. Many experiences in our lives come from behaviors that we choose based on the messages we believe. When I accept an empowering message from the Spirit of God as fact or truth, I act out of that perspective and continue on my spiritual path. When I accept a limiting message from the spirit *not* of God as fact or truth, I act out of that perspective (my limiting behavior) and thus my experiences of life take me off my spiritual path.

The acceptance of the message is a moment born of free will and discernment. Our own free will determines if we believe the information to be true or false, whether that message is from the Spirit of God or from the spirit *not* of God.

To assess the messages leading to your limiting behaviors, listen to your justifications for doing them. They may be justifications you tell others or yourself, but they are very persuasive. They can be so persuasive that you might think they are facts rather than messages. These are the ways I justify not being the person God is inviting me to be. These are the messages I hear in my head and believe in my heart.

My justification list looked like this:

My Limiting Behaviors	What I Tell Myself to Justify That Limiting Behavior
I waste time on the computer.	I am too tired to do anything productive.
I isolate myself.	No one else would understand or accept me.
I don't pray consistently.	OMG, like who has time to pray every day?
I spin thoughts in my head.	I'll be okay as long as no one knows what I'm thinking.
I lose my stuff all the time.	I am so scattered.
I eat too many sweets.	I have no willpower.
I don't speak up for myself.	It's not worth the conflict.

Now it's your turn. Just as quickly as you wrote your own list of behaviors, pin down how you justify those behaviors. You know your own behaviors and you know the messages in your head. Name the justifications that are holding you back. Don't judge yourself for making these justifications. You are just seeing the many justifications you offer for not being your best self. The reality that you make these justifications is a fact, but the justifications themselves and what they say about you are not factual. They are messages you are heeding.

Colloquy 10: My Limiting Messages

My Limiting Behaviors	What I Tell Myself to Justify That Limiting Behavior

Given the reality created by these limiting messages, how can you respond to God? You may often wonder why you are not as faithful or filled with consolation as you want to be. The reason for this is right in front of you. Being a co-laborer with God while holding such a limiting perspective of yourself is self-sabotaging; look closely at any one of your statements and imagine what it's like for you, trying to succeed with that kind of recording playing in your head. Ask yourself: With these perceptions of myself, what experiences am I going to have? Where do these messages lead me? Do any of these statements lead in the direction of wholeness? American writer Richard Bach, author of *Jonathan Livingston Seagull*, says, "Argue for your limitations and sure enough they'll be yours." The only benefit to believing these messages is the relief of not having to challenge them. Believing these messages does not lead you toward God.

In your mind share these justifications with your Walking Partner. You likely have heard each of them in your head many times, but there is one that you have come to accept as fact, one that you have given up any possibility of not acting out of. Yes, just one. Ask your Walking Partner which one of these is most limiting your progress on your spiritual path. You don't need to try to change everything you believe at once. Just be honest and name the one that has the most powerful hold on you. You know it. Your Walking Partner knows it.

You might hear a protesting thought, *No, not that one, pick any of them but not that one.* That would be the spirit *not* of God suddenly fearing losing a hold on you. In fact, if the justification message you picked doesn't really cause you angst to admit and instead feels like one that isn't really that big of a deal, you are probably avoiding the elephant in the room. Which message about yourself do you really buy into because it is just the way it is and will never change? In your mind, it is reality.

Write down that most powerful limiting message or justification for not being the person God created you to be. You are naming the chasm to leap over throughout the coming year.

Colloquy 11: The Most Powerful Limiting Message I Hear

Conversion of the Heart

To be a co-laborer with your Walking Partner, learn to hear what that voice inside you is saying, and then judge whether its messages are from the Spirit of God or the spirit *not* of God. To grow closer to God you need to choose, and continue to choose, which messages you are going to heed as Truth. Setting goals and planning ways to live out your faith when you are following the spirit *not* of God is like drawing up a map to a place you don't want to go. Instead, we embrace our free will and our agency to act as a collaborator with the Spirit of God that is always present, even though it is not always easy to hear among the clatter from the spirit *not* of God. For today, making this choice to confront the spirit-*not*-of-God message that you are falsely believing as truth is a one-time discernment, but to actually confront that message will take a daily, sometimes moment-by-moment practice of not acting out of its false premise.

Finally, do not gear yourself for a bruising battle. While Ignatius often spoke of his spiritual journey in terms of a battle, his ultimate goal was to surrender to the will of God, and to love in all his actions. Your ultimate goal is a sense of peace that you are on your spiritual path, collaborating with your Walking Partner. Often during Spiritual Path retreats, pilgrims would say what a sense of peace they felt just in articulating the deeply submerged, limiting messages that had been spinning in their heads for years.

This is the moment of transformation or conversion of heart. On your spiritual path you know there is a chasm just ahead. You are going to have to take a leap of faith. There is no way around it. There is no spiritual path that doesn't have a leap over a chasm. When you make this leap, you are saying "I don't believe you" to that spirit *not* of God because you are listening to the Spirit of God calling to your heart from the other side of the abyss. And in truth, it's not really an abyss you are leaping over; it is just a puddle. But that spirit *not* of God is going to tell you it is an abyss that you will never be able to climb out of if you try to leap forward from where you are. That spirit *not* of God is going to tell you this is not *where* you are, but *who* you are, and there is no way to change or override this message. Meanwhile, the Spirit of God is saying, "You, my beloved child, are my collaborator. You've got this. We've got this."

Standing on Solid Ground

To overcome that message from the spirit *not* of God, we reinforce ourselves with greater, undeniable truths. The messages of evil or of your being so limited are built on a foundation of sand. They are a façade. To tear down that façade, you need to have a stronger foundation upon which to stand.

Truth #1: The divine lives in you.

God is not above the clouds or in some ephemeral world beyond the confines of earth. The divine lives deep within each of us and speaks to us in the deepest desires of our heart. God is not separate from you; God is within you. Can you accept that?

Truth #2: The divine seeks that you be whole and fulfilled.

This is God's deepest desire. Whatever your Walking Partner looks like, that Partner is seeking your wholeness, not your destruction. If to love is to will the good of the other and God is Love, then God is willing what is truly good for you, that which will set you free and make you whole and most fully you. This is the acceptance that we are loved unconditionally.

Truth #3: You are a collaborator with God.

God is calling out to us constantly no matter what, longing to be closer to share the power of love and healing. But God doesn't control us or the people or world around us. God gives us freedom because to love must always be a free choice. We have to allow ourselves to be in this situation with God. Transformation can happen only when we are open to it and are ready to do our part to make it happen. Don't wait for God to do all the work of changing the world to fit you. You have to change or act with God to create a new situation.

There may be a voice inside you screaming really hard that those three truths are ridiculous. Maybe it is saying that this is just more religious mumbo jumbo. Maybe it is saying that this is so stupid, why would anyone believe or even think those things? Maybe it is saying, "This is going to swell your ego; don't buy into it." Whatever weakness you are prone to, that is where the spirit *not* of God will strike.

But maybe, just maybe, those three truths are real. Those truths are the foundation from which you leap to cross this chasm to challenge the spirit *not* of God. You already have the power to overcome that message of the spirit *not* of God that has for too long been limiting you and your dreams and deepest desires. This was the miracle of the Good News for those thought to be outside of God's love—the lepers, the prostitutes, the poor. Their acceptance of God's love is what Jesus meant by "your faith has healed you." Grounding our thinking in these truths leads to the interior freedom crucial for healthy discernment.

Rejecting the Spirit *Not* of God

Standing firmly on those three truths, confront the limiting message from the spirit *not* of God by flipping it completely upside down. What would the other side of that message sound like? The exact opposite.

Here are some examples from fellow pilgrims just to give you a better understanding:

Message I Hear from the Spirit Not of God	Freeing Message I Courageously Write from the Spirit of God
I'm too tired to do anything productive.	I am eager to get done what I am called to do.
No one will understand or accept me.	Others need to hear my voice.
OMG, who has time to pray every day?	Prayer is my first priority every day!
I'm so scattered!	I am so focused!
I'm okay as long as no one knows what I'm thinking.	I share exactly what I am thinking with those I love.
I have no willpower.	I protect my body.
I know it all.	I learn wisdom from others.

Ask your Walking Partner for enough courage to write the exact opposite message below. You are writing what you yearn for the situation to be instead of what it is now in your mind. Unlike your Signposts, this is not a piece of advice to be remembered or a new habit to form. This is your identity, your mantra declaring who you are as you walk this path. This is your heart's deepest desire, and it is God's desire for you, too! Don't limit the invitation the Spirit of God is offering you. Don't allow yourself to think it is impossible or silly. Let your statement say exactly what you desire for yourself. If it is a healthy desire that is going to lead you closer to God, it is God's desire for you too. In fact, it may be easier for you to hear it as your Walking Partner saying it to you because you don't really believe it—yet!

Colloquy 12: Flipping My Limiting Message
from the Spirit *Not* of God

Courageously write the freeing message I hear from the Spirit of God, a message that is the exact opposite of my limiting message.

My Walking Partner's response to this new Spirit of God message:

After articulating this freeing message from the Spirit of God, sit with the possibility its truth holds for your life. Note what is stirring inside: Hope that it just might be true? Fear that this is completely unknown territory for you? In his Rules for Discernment, St. Ignatius instructs us to boldly, courageously confront the enemy of our human nature, and it will wither. For now, you have just shined a spotlight on an untruth that has been limiting your response to the love of God, and you have turned your head to see what the opposite direction might look like. Next, you start walking your spiritual path in that direction, and you don't look back.

Claiming Your Sacred Mantra

A mantra is a word or sound that has special spiritual power. The *om* (pronounced OOOHMMMMM), probably the most well-known mantra, is meant to bring to those who repeat it a peaceful wholeness with the divine. But mantras don't have to be specifically religious words. All words have power because we give them power over us and our identity, essentially because we buy into them.

You can articulate your own sacred mantra that gives you power over that limiting message from the spirit *not* of God. Your mantra does not have to be musical or sung. Your mantra only has to be the message that names the Truth you embody. Your mantra will change over your lifetime as you live into some mantras and need new ones for new limiting messages. There is nothing magical about a mantra, but it can be extremely powerful because it is how we reclaim our own sacredness when it is questioned or challenged. Think of it as your compass for your spiritual path.

There is a formula for writing your own sacred mantra. Rewrite that flipped limiting message from Colloquy 12 so that it is:

- Personal;
- Present tense;
- Positive;
- Powerfully stated; and
- Pointing you to consolation.

Personal—That means using "I." This statement is about you; the message God is trying to get you to understand about who you are. If your statement is more about how you perceive the world, for now start it with "I live in a world that . . ." and then lay out the message that will lead you to God.

Present tense—God is in the present. Not the past and not the future. God is here and now, and you are and can only be your true self here and now, so your message from God is in the present tense. This is not that you will win the lottery, or you will someday be a doctor. This is a reframing. A new Voice telling you how it is right now. For example, "I have all the financial resources I need to thrive," or "I am a strong manager," or "I have what it takes to be a doctor right now."

Positive—Rather than focus on what not to do, the Spirit of God affirms what we are called *to do*. "You shall love the Lord your God with all your heart, and with all your soul, and with all your mind, and with all your strength . . . [and] love your neighbor as yourself" (Mark 12:30–31) are positive commandments. Flip any *don'ts* into positive affirmations. Instead of "I don't eat sweets," the message is "I eat healthy food that tastes good."

Powerfully stated—This is the part where you get to make it your own and hear how strongly the Voice of God believes in you. Use strong adjectives, insider messages that only you and your Walking Partner understand, or titles that give you power over your actions. *I eat healthy food* can be worded *I am the protector of my body's life source!*

Pointing you to consolation—God is not giving you a message or identity about your past or who you used to be. This is about your calling, where you are going on the Spiritual Path. This is your Magnificat, how your soul magnifies the Lord.

Try wordsmithing and rewriting that limiting-message-flipped-on-its-head to fulfill the criteria above. Keep working at it until you have the words that directly confront the message from the spirit *not* of God and stop it in its tracks. Hold each word gently and get input from your Walking Partner and even your fellow pilgrims. This is your Sacred Mantra.

Colloquy 13: Claiming My Sacred Mantra

Write your Sacred Mantra to meet the formula stated above.

My Walking Partner's response to what I shared:

Living into Your Sacred Mantra

You are being invited into this new identity. You didn't form it. God is ahead of you, inviting you in. If it feels laughable or a serious stretch to think about yourself as your Sacred Mantra declares, then you are on the right track. This is not just positive thinking. Remember the solid, prayerful, sacred ground you stand on. Given that ground, can you see how this is your Truth?

The example I like to use of growing into your new Sacred Mantra is the founders of the United States writing that statement in the Declaration of Independence, "All men are created equal." Never before had there been a country governed by law where all people were created equal instead of subjects of a sovereign, but the founders had imagined it. Once they put that statement into the Declaration, they had to live into it. They struggled, as we still do, with the full implication of it and how to implement it, but they knew in their hearts that it was the truth and very much reflective of a Higher Power. From the moment they signed the Declaration this became one of the sacred mantras of the United States. Even though we still struggle to live into it, we hold that mantra as sacred to our identity.

If you are saying to yourself, *This will take a miracle to pull off,* that is what the Spiritual Path is all about. A miracle just happened. You figured out what the Spirit of God desperately desires you to hear to be the collaborator you uniquely can be. Remember messages and thoughts lead to behaviors, and healthy behaviors lead to growth. This Sacred Mantra is your judgment about yourself before your action in any given situation.

Take some time to get this Sacred Mantra worded as you like. You can tinker with it, but only to make it more powerful, not less. When you think you have it, say it out loud as a statement of fact about yourself:

My name is . . . I live in . . . and [insert your new mantra here] . . .

This is going to feel very awkward. You are going to feel as if you are completely lying. Again, that is the spirit *not* of God trying to deny your true identity, your progress on your spiritual path. Your Sacred Mantra is your faithful internal compass.

Over the next year you are going to grow into this Sacred Mantra. Imagine you were just admitted to your dream college. You can legitimately claim you are now a Warrior or a Blue Jay or a Fighting Irish! It is true now and yet over the coming year you will grow into a clearer understanding of what this new identity means to you. Even so, you can proudly and legitimately take on your new mantra today.

Repeat your Sacred Mantra to yourself constantly. Share it with others proudly. You will acknowledge each month for how well you lived it out. You will hear so many messages from the spirit *not* of God negating this new mantra. When that happens, simply repeat the Sacred Mantra in your head. Say, "Thank you for sharing. Now go away," to that lame voice trying to lure you off your Spiritual Path, and then keep moving forward.

Act!

Now it is time to act. With full confidence that this is as much God's desire for you as it is your desire for yourself, write your Sacred Mantra on your Spiritual Path plan in the back of the book. This is a sacred act, and in performing this action, you embrace this new identity.

Reflect!

To complete another Cycle of Growth, take just a few minutes to reflect on your experience of defining a Sacred Mantra to confront the spirit *not* of God. Where was God in this experience? What have you learned that you are going to take with you? In what ways do the three truths—that the Divine lives within you, that the Divine seeks your wholeness and fulfillment, that you are a collaborator with the Divine—give you a solid foundation for this journey? Breathe deeply and immerse yourself in your Sacred Mantra. "Let it be with me according to your word" (Luke 1:38).

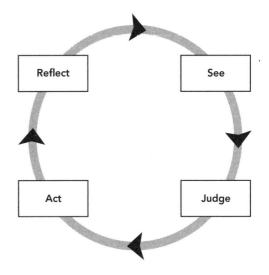

Colloquy 14: The Experience of Naming a Sacred Mantra

Share with my Walking Partner how this process unfolded for me.

My Walking Partner's response to walking through this Cycle with me:

Now you are ready to identify your unique Sources of Energy for this journey.

Chapter 7

What Are My Sources of Energy?

Naming Your Values and Strengths

Therefore, each particular being, in its individuality,
its concrete nature and entity, with all its own characteristics
and its private qualities and its own inviolable identity,
gives glory to God by being precisely what He wants it to be
here and now, in the circumstances ordained for it by
His love and His infinite art.

THOMAS MERTON

As you set your goals for the coming year on your Spiritual Path plan, there may be times when your journey gets a bit treacherous. There will be virtual headwinds when you feel as if people or systems are actively working against you. There will be times when the pathway feels gravelly and shifting. There will be times when you just don't have the energy and want to give up and go back to not working your plan. There are definitely risks to putting yourself out there to seek any goal—not just the risk of not reaching your goal but also the risk of losing confidence in yourself along the way. In this chapter we name those aspects of your identity that will give you the energy to keep going: your values and strengths. Values are abstract terms that represent your deepest-held beliefs about what fulfills your soul. Strengths reflect your natural capacity to act in any given situation. Every goal you set will be easier to reach if these energizers are at play.

Your values and strengths are utterly unique to you. No one else brings the same experiences, background, skills, passions, and perspectives to this calling. No one else is in this situation at this place and this time. Most important, no one else can be you or has that unique way of living out this desire in your heart. You, in your absolute uniqueness, make God dance!

By naming and acknowledging your values and strengths, you are saying this is how the divine is manifested in me. This is what I bring to the table. This is how I am gifted. You are not boasting. You are not putting others down for not having your strengths or values because in all humility you can easily admit that you do not possess other values and strengths that the world really needs. Thank God that God is manifested in so many different ways! Moreover, if you don't bring your values and strengths to the table as you are called, something will be missing that others need. If you use your values and strengths in setting your goals, you will often find an abundance of consolation. The situations themselves may not be easy at all, but you bring a confidence and capacity to them that comes naturally. When your strengths are not at play or are diminished by others, the path can be sluggish, and you begin to question how you should move forward. The key is to know your values and strengths and frame your role in a given situation to build on them.

Values as the Criteria for Your Goals

St. Ignatius noted that God's presence is with us in all experiences. Thus, we should not seek (not be attached to wanting) wealth or poverty, sickness or health, a long life or a short one. That is shocking for most people to hear. Is Ignatius telling us not to be healthy or not to be financially responsible? No. He is saying that we should not *get attached* to good health or wealth or a long life. This is not our identity. This is not what we are here to do. Too often we are attached to these outcomes and seek them instead of seeking to live through whatever situations we are facing with an awareness of our unique calling.

It is not easy to be detached from our human desires. Who doesn't want a long life rather than a short one? But if we are so attached to that desire for a long life that we are willing to compromise our values, we have denied the presence of God in the opportunity to thrive. If we don't prioritize our values, our desires can become an obsession, acting like a bulldozer driving us to mow over anyone and anything in order to obtain what we want. So while it is important to have goals, we need not compromise ourselves to reach them.

If we focus on our values instead of on outcomes, we begin to realize that life is more about the journey than the destination. We may succeed or fail to achieve our goals by conventional standards, but if we remain true to our values, then we will stay on our path. Many saints appear to have failed in their mission when they were killed, but they were actually remaining true to their values, even at the cost of their lives. What they were called to do was not a waste of time. Neither was it a test from God. But the world around them was not as open to live out those values as they were.

Identifying your values as criteria for your decision-making tends to cut off internal conflict before it starts. That does not mean it is easy! Living your values often leads you into conflict when others have different values in a situation. Focusing on shared values is the key to group cohesion. You may disagree on tactics for reaching a goal, but if everyone on a team respects one another's values, you can share common ground. The point of departure from a group or organization comes when you are asked to compromise your values. Regardless of the goal at hand, if the way it is being achieved goes against your values, you are veering from your spiritual path. Having real conversations or experiences with people who hold a set of values different from yours is a way to grow. If your values are too rigid, it is like driving on a narrow lane between two cement barriers. There is no room for error either on your part or on the part of anyone else sharing your path. Ignatius calls this living in the tension.

Identifying Your Values

So how do you identify your values? First, seek the grace of self-honesty. Don't allow fear or hesitation to limit you in this brainstorming. You are seeing which values resonate with you. Think about situations where these values were or weren't present and the impact that had on your sense of consolation or desolation. Be aware of the messages inside your head, and of the spirit *not* of God goading you to make a choice based on what other people might think of you. You may be thinking about the praise you will receive from others, even if the choice does not reflect one of your core values. Or you may be afraid to go against popular opinion and choose a stance that does reflect your values because you dread being criticized or belittled. Take a deep breath, say "Thank you for sharing," and, with the Spirit of God, claim the values that best reflect your heart without shame or fear. Consider what comes to you as you review the prompts and the list of values that follow in the next two-part colloquy.

Colloquy 15a: Values I Seek to Reflect

- What values are reflected in my lifestyle?

- What characteristics do I most admire in others?

- What really upsets me? (The opposite of that action or characteristic is often something you value dearly.)

- What do I want to be known or remembered for?

- What are my obsessive tendencies? What values do these tendencies point to?

- Think of a time of strong consolation. What values were at play at that time?

Colloquy 15b: The Values List

Circle the five values in the list that most resonate with you.

Values List [27]

Integrity
Accountability
Candor
Commitment
Dependability
Dignity
Honesty
Honor
Responsibility
Sincerity
Transparency
Trust
Trustworthiness
Truth
Feelings
Acceptance
Comfort
Compassion
Contentment
Empathy
Grace
Gratitude
Happiness
Hope
Inspiration
Irreverence
Joy
Kindness
Love
Optimism
Passion
Peace
Poise
Respect
Reverence
Satisfaction
Serenity

Thankfulness
Tranquility
Welcome
Spirituality
Adaptability
Altruism
Balance
Charity
Communication
Community
Connection
Consciousness
Contribution
Cooperation
Courtesy
Devotion
Equality
Ethics
Fairness
Family
Fidelity
Friendship
Generosity
Giving
Goodness
Harmony
Humility
Loyalty
Maturity
Meaning
Selflessness
Sensitivity
Service
Sharing
Spirit
Stewardship
Support

Sustainability
Teamwork
Tolerance
Unity
Achievement
Accomplishment
Capability
Challenge
Competence
Credibility
Determination
Development
Drive
Effectiveness
Empowerment
Endurance
Excellence
Fame
Greatness
Growth
Hard work
Improvement
Influence
Intensity
Leadership
Mastery
Motivation
Performance
Persistence
Potential
Power
Productivity
Professionalism
Prosperity
Recognition
Results-orientation
Risk

Significance	Calm	Restraint
Skill	Clarity	Rigor
Skillfulness	Concentration	Self-reliance
Status	Focus	Temperance
Success	Silence	Toughness
Talent	Simplicity	Vigor
Victory	Solitude	Will
Wealth	**Intelligence**	**Freedom**
Winning	Brilliance	Independence
Creativity	Cleverness	Individuality
Creation	Common sense	Liberty
Curiosity	Decisiveness	**Courage**
Discovery	Foresight	Bravery
Exploration	Genius	Conviction
Expressiveness	Insightful	Fearlessness
Imagination	Knowledge	Valor
Innovation	Learning	**Order**
Inquisitiveness	Logic	Accuracy
Intuitiveness	Openness	Carefulness
Openness	Realistic	Certainty
Originality	Reason	Cleanliness
Uniqueness	Reflectiveness	Consistency
Wonder	Thoughtfulness	Control
Enjoyment	Understanding	Decisiveness
Amusement	Vision	Economy
Enthusiasm	Wisdom	Justice
Experience	**Strength**	Lawfulness
Fun	Ambition	Moderation
Playfulness	Assertiveness	Organization
Recreation	Boldness	Security
Spontaneity	Confidence	Stability
Surprise	Dedication	Structure
Presence	Discipline	Thoroughness
Alertness	Ferocity	Timeliness
Attentiveness	Fortitude	**Health**
Awareness	Persistence	Energy
Beauty	Power	Vitality

Now is the time to huddle up with your Walking Partner. Between your answers to the initial values questions and the value words that most resonate with you, prioritize the five values that you are most willing to live by and be accountable to.

Colloquy 16: Naming My Values

Reviewing all the values I noted in Colloquy 15 *a* and *b*, which five values are the most important to me?

1.

2.

3.

4.

5.

My Walking Partner's response to these values I have identified to live by:

Do these values fit the person you are? Do they give you a sense of energy and endurance? These are the lines you are unwilling to cross in the coming year. If they are honestly what drives you, what you value, the Spirit of God will likely give you some sense of affirmation that this is who you are created and called to be. If in this colloquy you identify a value that is contradictory to your faith, that is definitely a topic for a good spiritual director conversation.

In this process of identifying your values, you have grown in self-awareness and self-honesty. One fellow pilgrim said, "I loved this process! It was a distillation, like a balsamic reduction of what matters to me." Notice the sense of consolation that alone brings. You are working to articulate and be the person you were created and called to be. Living these values is a big part of how you will praise, reverence, and serve God in the coming year.

Identifying Your Strengths

My Journey

For the better part of seventeen years, Saturday mornings were a source of tension in my house. For me, Saturday was the morning with no alarm! Sleep until you can't anymore. Let the kids get their own breakfast whenever they wake up. No stress! We have the whole weekend! But for my husband, although the alarm might not go off, Saturday was still a day to get up and get that task list done. Only after the grass was cut, the laundry was in and folded, the dog had been walked, the meals planned, and shopping completed for the upcoming week would there be any fun or relaxation. Neither of us understood what the other was thinking. Then, as part of my job running a leadership training program, I had to coach a participant on the findings from the Clifton *StrengthsFinder*.[28] This tool is one of many ways to identify a person's unique strengths. So, I asked my husband if he would be my guinea-pig client, take the online test, and let me be his coach. He agreed. When his top five strengths came back, our Saturday morning tensions quickly became clear. Among his top five strengths is one called "Activator," which means he is wired, by nature or nurture or the Holy Spirit, to get things done now! He is the anti-procrastinator. It's not that he loves to be busy all the time. It's not that he wants to see me suffer when he springs out of bed at 6:30 in the morning and it is still dark outside. Quite the opposite. He just can't relax until our task list is off his back. It took me seventeen years to see and name this annoying aspect of his behavior as a strength and a gift. Now that I had a name for it, I saw how it worked to my advantage in so many ways. He did a ton of stuff to keep our family going. If I could set up the situation using my organizational strengths to be framed around his activator strengths, life could be truly beautiful. Now, on Friday nights I can clarify what needs to be done for the weekend, being sure not to put too many tasks on our list, knowing he can't relax until the list is done. I can identify times when we both agree to get things done, and stick to it, so he trusts that we don't need to jump up first thing. Voilá! Mischief managed! Saturday morning's tension disappeared. Lots more consolation.

So did God make my husband an activator? I can't really say. What I can say is his capacity for getting things done is truly amazing. Not just little things like household tasks, but big things like writing articles and books and setting up ways for children to be fed or his students to do service. When he puts those strengths to work in a situation that reflects the love of God in some way, there is no doubt he is manifesting the divine.

Lest you think this is just my odd capacity for linking divine influence with business practices, Gallup itself had an entire division dedicated to strengths-based churches and parishes. The book *Living Your Strengths: Discover Your God-given Talents and Inspire Your Community* uses the exact same online *StrengthsFinder* tool offered in their corporate leadership training.[29] The authors added Scripture references to each strength, and anecdotes about the impact of using personal strengths on community. They directly attribute those strengths to the Holy Spirit.

This online tool is not the only way to identify your strengths. There are many other instruments used to understand personality (The Enneagram, Myers-Briggs Type Indicator, the DISC assessment, etc.) that offer insights into your strengths and gut reactions. If you can't easily name some of your strengths now, it pays to learn more about yourself before setting goals. The key to these types of personality tests is not just to take them and read the results but also to understand their implications for you. What does it matter that you are an ENTJ? Or Red? Or a 5 with a 6 wing? If you take these tests and put them on the shelf, you are missing valuable insights that could make your spiritual path more fulfilling.

Talk to the people around you about what strengths they see in you. The people who work and live with you every day know how you react in various situations, what they rely on you to do better than they can do themselves, and how you surprise them by how you approach certain situations. These all point to strengths that you naturally embody, probably without even trying. These are the same strengths you want to use on your spiritual path. Likely your strengths were at play in that list of consolations you identified earlier. Consider not only what activities you were doing but also the characteristics of your role during times of consolation. Were you the researcher, the organizer, the social connector, the strategist, the persuader, the aesthetics guru, or the cheerleader?

Everyone has strengths. These strengths reflect the Spirit of God uniquely manifested within us.

Colloquy 17: Identifying My Strengths

Consider the following prompts:

- I feel the most energy when I am . . .

- I could spend hours . . .

- Other people call on me to . . .

- When I start a new role or job, the first thing I want to do is . . .

- Am I more naturally the thinker, the doer, the power broker, or the glue that holds the team together?

- My natural inclination when I have free time is to . . .

- Other people say I am really good at . . .

- If asked to write an advice column for a newspaper, I would give people advice on how to . . .

- Looking back on my life, what did I do to get through the hard times?

- What can I not *not* do?

- What strengths do you recognize from other sources, such as personality tests?

Would your Walking Partner add any other strengths?

However you come to know and identify your strengths, now is the time to claim them. Trust that the world needs you to share them. Appreciate that you have been living out of them all along. Remember you are acting out of your Sacred Mantra. Next, in collaboration with your Walking Partner, list what you believe are your top five strengths.

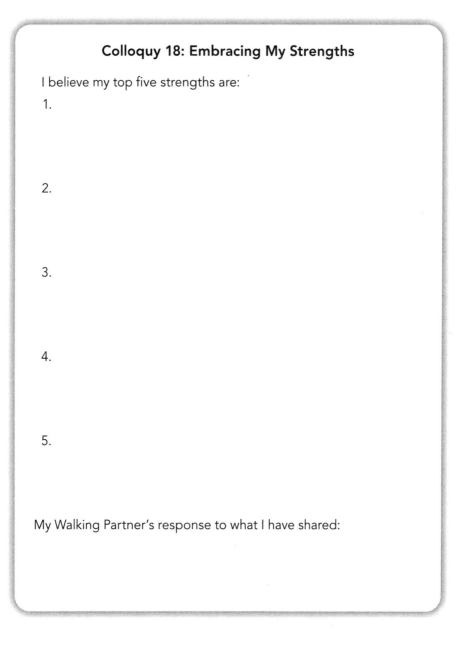

Colloquy 18: Embracing My Strengths

I believe my top five strengths are:

1.

2.

3.

4.

5.

My Walking Partner's response to what I have shared:

Notice that there are no negatives on this list. Negatives do not give us energy. In fact, focusing on deficits depletes our energy for reaching our goals. Out of thirty-four possible *StrengthsFinder* themes, Gallup consultants tell their leaders to focus on each individual's top five strengths. Since other people have their own top five, our deficits are counterbalanced when we are immersed in a diverse community. This is important to remember because over the next year there will be times when we need the strengths and capacities of others to help us reach our goals. No one finds fulfillment alone. Our deficits will be another pilgrim's strengths. Thus, we journey together.

To apply these strengths, you will set goals and objectives that are consistent with using them and then team with others to help in areas that aren't your strong suit.

Feeling the Wind at Your Back

Without having done this process before, you have been walking a spiritual path for years, learning and growing toward the person you are today. Along the way, you have developed your strengths and fortified your values. Rely on them now. These values and strengths are the energizers of your spiritual path.

There is a dark side to values and strengths that is a critical aspect of being self-aware. When we cling to a value to the detriment of others, when we aren't willing to accept the values of other people as relevant, or when we overuse our strengths to the point of not leaving space for others to make their contribution, that wind at our backs can turn as destructive as a hurricane. Even when we are in search of a well-discerned goal, our values and strengths can become hindrances if they become all-consuming.

You will likely feel some desolation when you realize you have let your values or strengths take precedence over another person. Remember, the ultimate goal here is to manifest the divine. To live life to its fullest as best you can. The ultimate goal is *not* to get to the end of the month and check all your boxes. That kind of goal is all ego, not love!

Naming Your Sources of Energy

You have seen the breadth of your possible values and strengths. A few have risen to the top in identifying who you are and what gives you the most energy. To keep these values and strengths in the forefront of your goal setting, you and your Walking Partner are going to choose just *three* that will keep you moving this year. Why only three? Because your top three are your strongest energizers, the ones most synonymous with your identity. Articulating these three ensures that you will not compromise yourself in pursuit of your goals.

Rest assured, you aren't losing your other strengths. You still value them, and they are still a part of how you are wired. If they aren't at play, you will likely feel a sense of desolation. Just prioritizing your values and strengths helps to make you aware of possible distractions and temptations to avoid in your goal setting.

Finally, before you make a final commitment to manifesting these Sources of Energy over the next year, know this isn't just talk. Each month of the coming year of your Spiritual Path plan, you will see and judge how well you lived these values and utilized your strengths. This is great for a discussion with a spiritual director or an accountability group.

For now, in the Judge phase of the Cycle of Growth, and in consultation with your Walking Partner, identify and list here the three Sources of Energy from your values and strengths lists (Colloquies 16 and 18) that you will rely on over the next several months. Any goals you set must first meet the criteria of using these Sources of Energy.

Colloquy 19: My Sources of Energy

Choose the three Sources of Energy from Colloquies 16 and 18 to be the initial criteria for my goals.

1.

2.

3.

Does my Walking Partner agree?

Like everything else on this journey, be gentle with yourself. You may claim one source of energy only to realize that you hold something else dearer. That is growth! You are free to come back to this chapter and reconsider your values and strengths. The key is to have your energizers in your back pocket.

Act!

The action in this Cycle of Growth is again to write down your Sources of Energy on your Spiritual Path plan. In doing so you are committing to being held accountable for living them as you pursue the goals you identify in the coming chapters. Feel the divinity within yourself as you complete this sacred act.

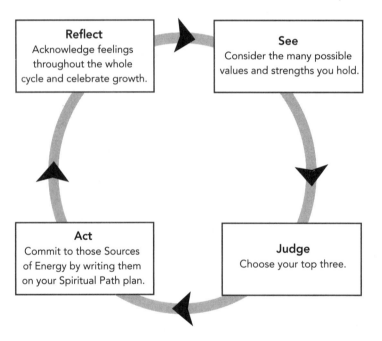

Reflect

For some people, identifying their own values and strengths is the hardest part of the journey. Celebrate and acknowledge what you have done. Notice the feelings that were inside of you as you read through the chapter, articulated your values and strengths, and chose the Sources of Energy that animate you.

Colloquy 20: What Did I Feel in Naming My Sources of Energy?

Where in this chapter did I experience the Spirit of God and the spirit *not* of God?

My Walking Partner's response:

If you accomplish nothing else in the coming year, you will still have made this world better through the strengths you manifested and the values you lived by. You are an amazing person just in who you are! There has never been nor will there ever be another you. It is crucial that you recognize this God-given uniqueness, beauty, and capacity in yourself. From this foundation of goodness embodied in you, your heart's desires will take flight.

You are deep into the wilderness of your soul at this point. Your honesty and willingness to let the process be your guide has brought you to some great scenic overlooks on your spiritual path. You have now completed the downward spiral of this Spiritual Path plan, the necessary pre-work and the self-awareness required to make healthy goals. This downward spiral of your Spiritual Path is in many ways the secret sauce of the process. It is where you have articulated your uniqueness in this relationship with God at this time and in the present context of your life. When you do a new Spiritual Path plan a year or six months from now, you may be surprised to see how much you have grown, and how much you have integrated what you learned from this plan, and how ready you are to go even deeper. So far you have:

- articulated useful lessons to smooth your spiritual journey;
- created a Sacred Mantra, a faithful internal compass; and
- identified your unique Sources of Energy for this journey.

You are also now familiar and comfortable with the See-Judge-Act-Reflect method for growth. The next segments of the journey will take multiple chapters to go through that cycle as you discern and commit to your goals by completing a one-page Spiritual Path plan.

Chapter 8

To What Relationships Am I Called?

Framing Your Spiritual Path

To love another person is to see the face of God.
VICTOR HUGO

By far, and across the board, when it comes to living their faith, let alone developing a Spiritual Path plan, the biggest frustration I hear from people is that they have too much to do! There is just not enough time! How can this be true when computers and other modern technology were supposed to make our lives so much easier? Social scientists once predicted the greatest problem of our time would be having too much leisure time and how to fill it. Instead, our dilemma is the exact opposite. We are wearing so many different hats that we have lost track of why we put on that hat in the first place!

Moving from a traditional approach of goal setting to a faith-based approach entails moving from a self-focus on achievement to a relationship-focus on calling. If you think about it, every role we play is really a relationship. Ultimately, God calls us to loving relationships, relationships of service. The main premise of Martin Buber's *I and Thou* is that the human life finds its meaningfulness in relationships and that all relationships lead us to relationship with God. Similarly, in his book *The Divine Dance*, Richard Rohr, OFM, helps us see that God is not an abstract, all-powerful entity to whom we pray; rather, God is the dynamic source that powers loving, compassionate relationships. Another way to understand relationship as the framework for our goal setting comes from Edward Kinerk, SJ. He notes that even though all desires are real, not all are "authentic" desires that emanate from, or are of, God. Kinerk writes, "In the final analysis, our desires and the energy they give are at the service of others."[30]

John Reid, author and facilitator of strategic planning for Catholic organizations, explains, "Planning is about more than problem solving. It is about building relationship, partnership, creating new possibilities, discovering gifts, planting seeds, designing new tapestries which will serve tomorrow well."[31] On a spiritual path, goal setting is not about personal achievement but rather personal growth through relationship.

This idea of relationships being key to our growth is not just spiritual theory. The interrelatedness between relationships and personal growth has been validated by research conducted at the Science of Learning Center, which is under the auspices of the United States National Science Foundation. Researchers describe the brain as "socially gated," which means that the brain is affected by the social environment. Our brains are both restricted, or negatively impacted, and enhanced, or positively impacted, by our interpersonal relationships. Social gating means that social interaction is essential for how each person grows into the person they are capable of being. Obviously, how a person is or is not nurtured as a child is critical to personal growth and identity. The idea that all our relationships shape who we are and how we act, however, is too often ignored in our culture, which tends to focus on being *self-made*. Notably, it is not just that others have an effect on us, but also that we choose our responses and reactions *in relation to* our circle of influence. The choice to be in relationship with someone and how we behave within that relationship is within our control as adults. The point here, however, is that, neurologically, our identities are in large part framed and formed by our relationships.

Meeting God in Relationships

The relationships to which you are called provide the framework for the goals on your Spiritual Path plan. Through these relationships, you have multiple paths to grow closer to God; multiple options for growing into the person you are called to be. What's important to remember is that it is *within these relationships* that the Spirit is present in the world both *to* you and *through* you.

Your spiritual path began years ago in the web and context of your relationships. You were born into a certain family and culture and era, and then, along the way, you made choices about which other relationships you would cultivate.

Whether you discerned and selected these relationships or just fell into them, they are, for now at least, a starting point that may or may not propel you toward God. As you walk your path, you may be called to add new relationships or end old ones. On your Spiritual Path, you will find that your goals will flow from the relationships that enable you to be more fully you, and thus better able to serve God.

Your role in your family is to be in relationship with your spouse, children, parents, siblings, or members of your extended family. Your role at work is the relationship between you and your supervisors, coworkers, clients, or the public at large that you are serving through your products and services. Being a member of the school PTA involves being in relationship with school administrators and other parents, all of whom agree to work toward common goals. Christ said clearly, "For where two or three are gathered in my name, I am there among them" (Matthew 18:20). To find where God is in your life, start by looking at your relationships, because it is here that you are called to be the face of God for others, and they are called to be the face of God for you.

The relationships framing your spiritual path aren't just one-on-one. Doing what you love or have been given a talent to do can be God's way of calling you to relationship with the wider world or with others who share your passion. A violin player is giving a gift to all who hear what she plays. That is a relationship with anyone listening. An activist fighting for justice for immigrants is in relationship with both immigrants she has never met and also with her fellow citizens whose country will be shaped by her influence. The gardener or the naturalist, seemingly alone in their pursuits, honors nature and seeks insights in a relationship with the natural forces of the world. These relationships where people give from their heart are among the most powerful ways God infuses the world with goodness. Identifying how you are gifted and called to be in relationship with the broader world invites us to another space for honest discernment. You will need to discern if what you spend your time doing is an escape from the world or a gift to the world.

One relationship everyone has is with ourselves as our own caretakers. Being our own caretaker means honoring our physical, mental, and spiritual health. Taking care of ourselves is vital to walking a spiritual path. When we do something that gives us joy, we are healthier and better able to deal with the challenges that inevitably will come. Mother Teresa insisted that every Missionary of Charity take regular (daily, weekly, monthly, annual) breaks from their work to get away and recharge. How is your relationship with yourself? What are you doing to care for yourself? God gave us life so that we might have it abundantly. What are the things you are doing to live abundantly?

As you begin to consider all the relationships that presently fill your days, don't be afraid to make room for a new relationship that has been waiting to be acknowledged. Maybe it is connecting with a person you haven't had the courage to go deeper with. Maybe it is a new hobby or profession you would like to try. Even though I had written dozens of blogs and reflections, I never saw myself as an author until I named it as one of my relationships with the world. Putting that down on my Spiritual Path plan gave me a new identity and established a new type of relationship, a new role to play, within the broader world.

Sometimes our hearts desire a relationship that is missing from our lives. Someone we haven't met yet. Naming a healthy desire for a relationship is an honest way to specify a path for moving closer to God. God is in that desire. You can't plan your way into meeting the person of your dreams, but you can set a goal to put yourself into situations where relationships of substance can blossom.

At Christmas, our family tracks the names of people who have come into our lives during the previous year and left their mark upon us in some way. I am continually amazed by the way our lives are shaped by people we didn't even know just a short time ago. Leaving space on your Spiritual Path plan for new relationships positions you with freedom to be curious and accepting about how God might be calling you. If you feel a desire in your heart to open your life to new relationships, name that. Leave space, time, and energy for whatever invitations may arise.

Note as well that we have relationships with pets and inanimate objects. As for our relationships with money, our homes, cars, work product—being tied in relationship to all of these things can shape our becoming. We can have healthy and unhealthy attachments to all of these components of life. Unlike relationships with people, though, relationships with objects don't lead to love.

Ignatius's teaching was clear: we are to use all the things of the earth to the extent that they move us closer to God; we are to let them go to the extent that they move us away from God.[32] The time you dedicate to your relationship with nonhuman objects or creatures is time you are taking from human relationships. That may be okay if those intervals make you healthier in body, mind, or spirit. The relationship may not be okay if you use this nonhuman object as an escape from or a replacement for human relationships. Ignatius would say we don't need to devalue or deny these relationships that have become disordered attachments; what we do need to do is reorder their prominence in our lives.[33]

Finally, before you identify the relationships to which you are called, consider naming two specific relationships in which the Spirit of God thrives, and allow the Spirit to stir them up a bit in your imagination before you judge whether or not they should be a part of your Spiritual Path.

The first type of relationship in which the Spirit of God flourishes is a relationship with people who are marginalized. This can take many forms, from working with people who are materially, socially, or spiritually struggling, to working for systemic change that helps alleviate the burdens placed on marginalized populations in society. The areas of human need in our community are endless, from hunger and illness, to addiction and isolation, to domestic violence and injustice. Jesus was clear in his call for every one of us to care for the least of those among us. For some, this may be a part of their paid work. For others, it may be as a volunteer. Or, as someone who is marginalized yourself, you may realize a goal to enhance your relationship with others in similar situations so as to be in greater solidarity with them. Often in our culture we distance and insulate ourselves from the pain of poverty. Jesus taught that being in relationship with the poor and broken is what brings wholeness to our lives (see Matthew 25:31–46). To engage with the poor may be out of your comfort zone. That's okay. Just be open to naming a relationship with the marginalized as part of your spiritual path. Whatever form this relationship may take, it is truly one of the most certain paths toward growing closer to God. Our divine nature moves us to respond to others when we allow ourselves to be in relationship with someone in need.

The second type of relationship in which the Spirit of God thrives is a relationship with the natural world. Pope Francis's signature encyclical *Laudato si'*, *On Care for Our Common Home*, beautifully calls all people to a relationship of compassion with the earth and all its creatures. The Bible prioritizes creation as a reflection of God's presence. Jesuit poet Gerard Manley Hopkins's most often-quoted poem opens with a line that zings its way straight to our hearts: "The world is charged with the grandeur of God."[34] In meditation we use recordings of birds or waves or wind or rain to calm our hurried minds. Time spent in the beauty of nature is good medicine for any human condition. We are all called to see ourselves as creatures within God's creation. How do you see yourself in that relationship? Perhaps as a protector? An advocate? A teacher? A collaborator? An embracer? There are many ways to be in relationship with the natural world, and honoring that relationship is a vital way to connect with the Spirit of God.

Nowhere in these relationships is it necessary to name a relationship with God specifically. In fact, one of the strongest motivations for this process came from the experience of people compartmentalizing their faith into just one role on their annual goal plans rather than recognizing God as present in the many relationships in their lives. If you do discern a desire in your heart for a deeper personal spiritual connection to a Higher Power, the best way to connect is through your relationship as your own caretaker. Just as no one else manages your mind and body, no one else controls your relationship with God. That is an intimate part of your identity. If you already have a strong sense of connection to a Higher Power, you will likely know if you need to prioritize more intentional time or a specific goal beyond what you already do to nurture that relationship. For now, know that God is present in all these relationships, so there is no need to call out a relationship specifically with God. In later chapters, as you identify goals, there will be plenty of space and grace to grow your personal connection to God via these relationships.

Seeing Many Paths to God

All the relationships in your life that require your time and attention are important to *see*. Before you set any goals, you will narrow down this list to those relationships that will help you most to grow during the coming year. For now, though, you are *seeing*, as an outside observer in conversation with your Walking Partner, the many relationship invitations you hold inside your heart. Your list may include individual relationships or a collective relationship with a group. The categories below may help inspire your list of relationships.

- **Family relationships:** spouse, parent of, child of, sibling, extended family, collectively or individually
- **Work relationships:** clients, supervisors, colleagues, direct reports, potential clients
- **Community relationships:** faith community relationships, neighborhood, city, state, federal, global
- **Activity relationships:** club or organization member, volunteer, hobby/practice
- **Desired friendship, caretaker, significant other**
- **Relationships with people who are marginalized**
- **Relationships with creation**

In this next colloquy, you will name the relationships you will prioritize in the coming year. Don't forget to name at least one relationship for taking care of yourself, the poor or marginalized, and the natural world.

During this process, remember that brainstorming is not judging. It is naming, seeing, and admitting the reality in which you and your Walking Partner are going to interact. Do not let the spirit *not* of God deter you from naming a relationship that is on your heart. Do not be afraid of having to make a commitment to a relationship. That is the work of discernment to come. For now, name the relationships you may be called to prioritize in the coming months. Be aware of what moves in you as you name them.

Colloquy 21: What Relationships *Might* Frame My Spiritual Path? (Step 1 of 4)

My caregiver:

My relationship with others who are marginalized:

My relationship with the environment:

Other relationships I may be called to in the coming months:

My Walking Partner's response to this list of relationships:

What a gift it is that God offers us so many paths to wholeness, so many with whom to share our journey, and so many ways to experience consolation. While every relationship can't be a priority, each is a gift to your soul.

Choosing Your Priority Relationships

Now comes the work of discerning which of those relational paths will take priority in the coming months. Review your list with your Walking Partner. Ask your Walking Partner's advice in pulling out the eight most important relationships your heart desires.

Discernment entails being honest as you reflect on what is churning inside your heart and mind. Is claiming this relationship as a priority in your life moving you closer to God? Is it giving you a sense of consolation in the form of hope, joy, love, eagerness, laughter, fulfillment, justice, rightness, and goodness? Does this relationship, or will this relationship, help you grow? Even though relationships of consolation can be challenging, your heart will affirm the rightness of their hold on you.

Or does claiming this relationship as a priority in your life give you a sense of desolation? Of feeling further from God? If you are prioritizing a relationship out of guilt, vanity, fear, or expectation, those are not of God. Do not consider removing the priority to take care of yourself since no one else can do this; it is not being selfish to make taking care of yourself a priority in your life as long as it is not the only relationship you are focusing on. Having at least one goal of taking care of yourself is a requirement on the Spiritual Path.

Neither can family relationships be denied as a priority. Marriage and parenthood present ongoing family responsibilities. For me, taking care of my aging parents was a relationship that was, at times, trying. Even so, I knew without hesitation that, at that time, I, more than anyone else, was being called to perform this role. Ignatius noted that we may have vows or obligations from which we cannot be released, including parenthood, marriage, and life vocations. These must take priority on your spiritual path, but they are not the whole of your spiritual path. If these vowed relationships truly are vocations, then they are your clearest paths to being the person you are called to be, and you feel a sense of consolation when you claim them as a priority for the coming year. If, in prioritizing these vocational commitments, you feel a sense of dread, angst, or weariness, listen to this: our vocations are not meant to be burdens—even though they may not always be easy. Vocations are challenging to maintain since they change over time as we grow into different people. The vocation of parenthood changes significantly between when children are newborns and when they go off to college. Be alert to the possibility that in naming a vocational relationship as a priority for your Spiritual Path plan, it is possible you are being called to address something within you that has become a source of desolation.

Family relationships as well as a particular family member can be considered a priority. Rather than identify each of my relationships with my children individually as the framework for my Spiritual Path plan, I identified being a mother to all my children as one of my eight priority relationships. I realized that throughout the year one child or another may take priority on my time and focus, but overall, my vocation was to raise a healthy family and ensure a safe home for everyone. Alternatively, there was a time when my daughter was a senior in high school and needed me to walk closely with her as she transitioned to being an independent adult. In this case, I named my relationship directly with her as one of my priority relationships. That doesn't mean I forgot my other kids. I simply knew they did not need as much intentional, personal focus.

Conversely, not prioritizing a relationship may be freeing, but it doesn't mean you completely lose that connection. You may have hundreds of Facebook or Instagram friends, but they can't all be your priority. Here, you are discerning which relationships God is calling you to prioritize in the coming months. An invitation to grow may come from any of these relationships or from relationships yet to be established. But as humans we are limited by time. We can't be all things to all people. Writing your Spiritual Path plan gives you a guide for being more intentional about how you use your time.

Ignatius also taught us to be aware of the temptation to the good. That is a way the spirit *not* of God works to draw us off our spiritual path by making us think something is really good or better than our heart's deepest desire. Sometimes we see this temptation to the good when we feel we need to do things, even nice things, for the wrong reason. It may be for the sake of appearances or for checking a box or because that's what "good" moms, dads, employees, neighbors, etc., do. These societal expectations are not to be confused with invitations to growth that come from God. In fact, they tend to clutter our calendars with hollow tasks that take our time away from what we are called to be doing. We can free ourselves from these temptations to the good by discerning where we are being called and allowing these other roles, responsibilities, and relationships to take a back seat, at least until, perhaps down the road, we discern that we are called to continue making them part of our growth.

In discerning the relationships that will shape your spiritual path, you are being proactive and acknowledging the invitations you have in your heart. As new invitations come in the form of new relationships over the coming year, you are free to consider how they stir you in light of the relationships you have already identified as your Spiritual Path framework. We hold these priority relationships gently rather than grasp them tightly. They are temporary gifts. Any of them may be taken from us on any day. Humanity is, if nothing else, a temporary existence. In that, there is grief and pain, but all the more reason to prioritize these relationships and allow them to affect us while they can.

You have, at best, eight relationships on which you can intentionally focus as places of growth in moving toward God in the coming year. And identifying a relationship as one of your top eight does not mean it will become a priority on your Spiritual Path. For now, you are weeding out those relationships that take energy away from who you were created to be. Some people complain that eight is too limiting. Keep in mind that you will set goals and pursue growth in each of these relationship areas. This chapter began with a reminder that lack of time is a common complaint for goal setting. We set ourselves up for desolation if we demand too many opportunities to pursue growth. Trust that God has colored your world plenty with these relationships you choose.

If you don't have eight, that's fine. Sometimes fewer is better. That leaves space for new relationships to be added to your spiritual path throughout the year.

Before you use this list, name these priority relationships in ways that reflect who you are in them. This is an opportunity to put on your creative cap. In the Bible, to name something meant you brought life to it. As you walk your spiritual path, you will bring life to these relationships. They should be named in a way that motivates you to bring new life to them. They can also be names that mean something only to you. Rather than just "mother," I see myself as "Mom and imparter of wisdom to Lem, Andrew, Michael, and Cate." I was not just "daughter," but "Mom's caretaker and companion in her final years." If need be, you can refine these names later, but for now, name each relationship so that it reflects its meaning to you spiritually.

Finally, keep in mind that this discernment emanates from your Sacred Mantra. Repeat it in your mind and say it to your Walking Partner as together you claim the priority relationships that will frame your Spiritual Path.

For Colloquy 22a, write the valiant name that is descriptive of each relationship. The order does not matter. In the next section we will look at the rating and reasons.

Colloquy 22a: Naming My Priority Relationships Valiantly (Step 2 of 4)

Identify which of the relationships from Colloquy 21 will be priorities on your Spiritual Path plan and then name them valiantly.

Colloquy 22b: Relationship Ratings and Reasons (Step 3 of 4)

Relationship 1 (Your name for your relationship with yourself.) _____

Rating: _____ Reasoning:

Relationship 2 _____

Rating: _____ Reasoning:

Relationship 3 _____

Rating: _____ Reasoning:

Relationship 4 _____

Rating: _____ Reasoning:

Relationship 5 _____

Rating: _____ Reasoning:

Relationship 6 _____

Rating: _____ Reasoning:

Relationship 7 _____

Rating: _____ Reasoning:

Relationship 8 _____

Rating: _____ Reasoning:

Give a big exhale as you review the relationships to which you are called on your spiritual path. Consider what was easy for you and what was challenging in coming to this list. In the movie *Schindler's List*, Oskar Schindler recognizes that the names of people on his list to be saved are far more than just words on paper. So it is for you, too. These relationships are priorities in your life, whether with spouses or children, readers, or entire generations, and yes, even with yourself and your own body. These are your circle of influence. We spend so much of our time tracking influencers and world events, but these personal relationships are the reality you are called to impact every day, week, or month on your spiritual path. These are where your soul resides.

Remind yourself of your Sacred Mantra and take a moment to share your gratitude with your Walking Partner for these relationships.

Checking Out the Terrain

On this Spiritual Path, your relationships can be likened to the terrain at any given moment. Some relationships are full of love and mutual support, and it is as if you are on a hovercraft to heaven. Others are really rocky, and it's difficult to experience the love of God in that relationship. Some relationships are on the uphill, as you are still trying to get to know the other person. Some relationships are like a downhill slope, easy and carefree, requiring little effort to move closer in intimacy and solidarity.

Before identifying goals for the coming year, now is the time to assess the condition of the road surface in each relationship. Rating a relationship is simply a numerical way for you to articulate what you see. It may feel like judging, but actually you are only naming reality as you see it. Rating something is a way to quantify the intangible, to benchmark where you are starting so that you can keep track of your growth.

Keeping your Sacred Mantra in mind, you are going to use a scale of one to ten and rate how you currently live out each relationship as a reflection of the person God created you to be. Intimacy with God is allowing God's will into each moment and interaction and living out that relationship. In this way, *Thy will be done* becomes concrete. If you're totally confident you are doing

God's will with how you are showing up in a relationship, give yourself a ten. A rating of ten would be the best you could possibly be, given the players involved and the situation. A ten would mean there is no room to grow deeper in that relationship. If you are fifty percent satisfied with how you are living out your call in a relationship, rate yourself a five. If you are not doing anything with a relationship or feel that you are engaging in the relationship in a way inconsistent with your personal values and calling, rate yourself at one. This is your own rating scale, so your idea of fulfillment in a relationship might be very different from someone else's. Thus, don't compare your ratings to anyone else's.

Being honest about where we are now in a relationship allows you to set realistic goals. In some relationships you might move from a one to a three over the course of a year. I once had a friend who had no desire to speak with her ex-husband, so her spiritual director suggested she consider praying for the desire. They compromised on praying for the desire to pray for the desire to someday speak with him again. That's growth! Rarely will people go from completely disparaging a relationship to completely honoring it. Sometimes our most challenging relationships or callings are the most important ones for our own spiritual growth. Keep in mind that mutual relationships are a two-way street. You can control only your part. Thus, setting goals that are out of your control will be setting yourself up for failure. You can invite others to be with you in achieving a level of intimacy and trust, but if they are unable to join you, be ready to hold yourself to the desired standard just the same.

As with any assessment, it is also important to acknowledge what is going well. In those places where you have the healthiest relationships, you will find the most support for walking the spiritual path. It is important to identify those wells of faith to nurture yourself.

As a reference point for benchmarking, after you rate each relationship, write a brief description of why you gave it the rating you did. Again, you are describing what you see without judgment or angst. This is your reality, and you and your Walking Partner are in it together.

Below is an example of what a rating and explanation might look like for a few relationships.

My Ratings and Reasons

- Relationship 1: Tom's soulmate. Rating: 8. Right now things are going really strong with us. We are finally in the place we need to be financially, so less stress is adding to our more positive dynamic. Over the past year I have relied on him for so many things, and he has come through every time. Always times I could be more attentive but feeling pretty good.
- Relationship 2: Mom and imparter of wisdom to Lem, Andrew, Michael, and Cate. Rating: 5. I feel as if I am adequate right now in my relationships with my kids. Times are crazy busy, and the kids are doing okay, but parenting at this age is not at all what I had expected. Could be better, could be worse!
- Relationship 3: My daily homies. Rating: 7. I love my team at work, but we don't make enough time to support each other personally. Sometimes I feel as if I barely know what is going on in their lives. This relationship could be stronger with more intentionality on my part, but I know at heart they are great people.

And so on for each of your eight priority relationships.

Now it is your turn. Remember, you are speaking out of your Sacred Mantra in conversation with your Walking Partner. Allow that perspective to permeate your rating, and honestly assess where you stand at the start of this journey. You don't have to go into elaborate detail; write just enough to confirm and remember why you gave that rating. This rating will also help you to set appropriate goals for each relationship going forward, as you begin to see what serious growth in any one relationship will require.

Go back to complete Colloquy 22b before continuing.

Whole Life Review

Your Spiritual Path plan will be comprised of goals you discern for each of your prioritized relationships. The diagram on the next page looks at these relationship ratings in context with one another. Over the next year, you are seeking to grow in each of these relationships; however, some relationships may need greater effort or focus than others. Visualizing your relationship ratings with this Whole Life Review allows you to see more easily where you are off balance in life. It also makes it easier to be honest about how much you think you can grow in each relationship in the coming year. This is the culmination of the See phase of this Cycle of Growth.

I have shared my Whole Life Review below to give you a sense of how to plot yours, and then connect the dots.

Whole Life Review

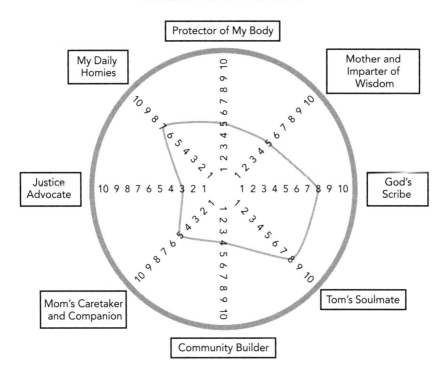

Colloquy 23: My Whole Life Review

Label the eight priority relationships with the corresponding name and rating you assigned to each. Then connect the dots.

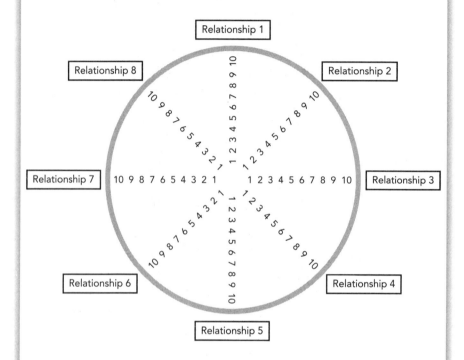

How does my Walking Partner respond to this diagram of my current life?

This shape represents your current reality. There is no judgment, just a visual representation of your world of influence. Obviously, the shape will look different depending on which relationships are next to each other. The point is to consider all your priority relationships in light of each other. Imagine how you would like that shape to look by the end of the year.

Identifying Your Greatest Invitation for Growth

Realistic goals for growth come from a review of where you are as you start on your Spiritual Path plan. Don't expect to go from crawling to running in a few months. But that journey starts somewhere. God meets us where we are. In any of your goals you can grow to be more the person you are capable of being, more the face of God, and thus closer to God yourself.

There is one relationship on the list above that is on your heart right now, however, and it is your Greatest Invitation for Growth toward God. It is not necessarily the one you rated the lowest. You may be satisfied just holding that relationship steady. It is not necessarily a new relationship you are starting if you just want to get your feet wet. It is not necessarily the relationships you are expected to prioritize such as your spouse or parent, because some years those people we love the most really need us to grow in new ways for ourselves instead of doting on them. Somewhere on that list, God invites you to give your time in the coming year to focus on one relationship. It does not mean the other relationships will suffer and not receive your time or attention. It just means you acknowledge with God that your deepest heart desire is urging you to pick this relationship as your Greatest Invitation for Growth.

Now you are moving into the Judge phase of this Cycle of Growth. Before discerning that Greatest Invitation for Growth, consider the following questions:

- Where is my life out of balance?
- If I could put one problem behind me once and for all, what would it be?
- In which relationship do I want a breakthrough in growth or depth?
- If I could put a big check by one of my relationships at the end of the next year, showing that I felt really good about how I'm engaging the other person, which one would it be?
- Is there a new relationship that I want to have a greater influence on my becoming?

In the next colloquy you will use the answers to these questions to help you select the one relationship that will be your Greatest Invitation for Growth this year. Naming one as your major focus helps you to prioritize, to have courage to go the distance, and to make the extra effort when it is most needed. When push comes to shove, the goals you set for this relationship will take priority. Each month you will score this relationship first and set goals for it with all other goals working around those. Choose the relationship in which you would like to make a major improvement in your capacity to be the person you are called to be. Don't be afraid to identify one of your personal relationships (personal manager, your hobby, etc.) as your Greatest Invitation for Growth. If that is your heart's desire and a clear invitation for you to become more whole and balanced, then that is God's desire as well.

Ignatius taught that God speaks in the healthy desires of our hearts. Determining if your desire is healthy often means sharing those desires openly with others and praying for grace to imagine yourself in that relationship. Can you do that? Does identifying this invitation for growth give you energy and joy, or fear and angst? Be wary of *shoulds*. Discern whether the invitation to grow in a relationship, possibly taking you out of your comfort zone, is an invitation to growth toward God or an invitation to guilt, desolation, and self-diminishment. Keep the focus on your invitation to grow.

Choose quickly by circling the relationship you feel is your Greatest Invitation for Growth. You probably already know which one it is. Is your Walking Partner in agreement?

Colloquy 24: My Greatest Invitation for Growth
(Step 4 of 4)

My Greatest Invitation for Growth:

My Walking Partner's response to this choice:

And . . . Action!

When you are ready to commit to your Greatest Invitation for Growth, take a deep breath and then write it on your Spiritual Path plan at the back of the book. This is a sacred act of commitment that this relationship will be a primary focus for the coming year. Know the Spirit of God is with you, working through you. There is nothing to fear.

Moving Higher and Higher (Really Wider and Wider!)

You may feel you have come a long way in naming reality and growing closer to the person you are called to be since beginning this process. You learned valuable lessons from the past year and wrote Signposts to keep you on your path going forward. With your Sacred Mantra you have put on a new identity that you are now living out, no longer letting that spirit *not* of God have a hold on your becoming. You have stocked up your Sources of Energy by naming your values and strengths. Finally, you have identified all the relationships to which you are called in the coming year and rated how you can traverse those relationship dynamics to be the person you are called to be. Now you know the one relationship to which you are being invited to significant growth. You are getting close to the top of the mountain where you will have a clear view of your spiritual path for the coming year.

To complete this Cycle of Growth, take time to reflect on how it felt to frame your Spiritual Path through your relationships, and what you learned in the process. Are you getting a better sense of how to practice the See-Judge-Act-Reflect method? Articulate the emotions you feel in the process as you continue to gain clarity about your calling.

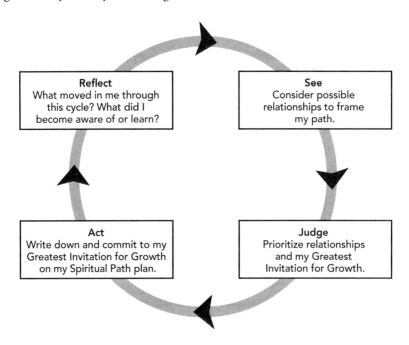

Colloquy 25: Reflection on Framing My Spiritual Path

Where did I sense movement or growth through this cycle? What did I become aware of or learn? Am I becoming more aware of my Walking Partner's presence in my life?

My Walking Partner's response:

Chapter 9

What Is Possible with God?

Imagining the Life to Which You Are Called

Whatever you vividly imagine, ardently desire, sincerely believe,
and enthusiastically act upon must inevitably come to pass.

PAUL J. MEYER

Now it is time to prime the pump before we delve into the goal setting for your Spiritual Path. St. Ignatius believed that one of the most powerful ways to pray or listen to God was through our imaginations. In fact, he was on his sick bed when he first imagined himself as a warrior for God. And yet he never could have imagined those dreams resulting in the largest worldwide order of priests and the education of millions of people over the course of five centuries. He never had to imagine all of that. He just imagined himself in total service to God in the context in which he was living. He put himself in the scene of his imagination, felt the actions he would take, observed how others responded, had entire conversations with others in the scene, and, most important, observed what that experience of imagining did to his spirit. When sitting with people and having spiritual conversations he would ask them to imagine Jesus in the chair across the room and what they imagined Jesus was saying to them. One of his most powerful forms of prayer is for a person to read a scene in the Gospels and then imagine themselves somewhere in that scene. Ignatius believed strongly that God speaks through the desires of the human heart as manifested in the imagination. According to my dear friend and parish priest, the late Pat Malone, SJ, "Saint Ignatius knew that what often blocks human growth is not a lack of will, but a lack of imagination of how good life is intended to be." For years John Reid, whom we met in the previous chapter, led parish groups in strategic planning. He writes in his book *The Art of Change*, "They [prophets] did not magically foretell the future, but prepared the people in the present for the future [that our hearts desire"].[35] Imagining our future best selves is where any pilgrim can be prophetic.

Looking at the relationships you identified in the previous chapter, what is possible with God? This is by far my favorite question on the Spiritual Path. Imagining your relationships is similar to an artist creating art. This is your future picture, so no one can tell you if it is accurate. That is between you and God. But you have a spiritual sense of whether the things you imagine draw you toward or away from God. Based on the discernment of the previous chapter and the relationships you want to prioritize in the coming year, this question asks you to imagine the best-case scenario for each relationship in the coming year. Start with your Sacred Mantra, stay firmly grounded in your best self, and go through each relationship with your Walking Partner. What might growth in that relationship look like? What state of being is possible in this relationship six months or a year from now? How does each ideal relationship look when enacted? Be as descriptive as possible. And, yes, I know: these images can go on for pages.

Here is a sample of what might come from imagining what is possible with God.

- In my relationship with my mom, I am called to respond to her with compassion and patience and seek ways to bring her joy. I can imagine leaving my time with her being confident that I am making the right decisions for her. I can imagine taking her to places and being a safe place for her to vent. I will ensure that she . . .
- In my relationship as an administrator, I am called to be organized and motivating. I can imagine myself as a servant leader who gently asks hard questions, holds others accountable, and creatively grows the organization. I will feel the most whole in this role when my team feels empowered to do their jobs with less stress. I can imagine the new program serving so many people and my staff being recognized for . . . Sitting at my desk, I focus on . . .
- In my relationship with my husband, I am called to . . . I can imagine us . . . My heart leaps when we . . .

In your imagination you are safe and free. You can let your Walking Partner lead. Something may pop up that you didn't expect. That's okay. Just write it down. But first, there are a few guidelines for this imaginative colloquy.

Avoid Riches, Honor, or Pride.

If you are imagining, *I will win the lottery so that I can build my dream home with a swimming pool*, you may need to consider which Spirit that idea is coming from. If your message has to do with obtaining more riches, honor, or pride, you might need to check whether you are being called by the Spirit of God or the spirit *not* of God. Ignatius says these are the telltale calling cards of the spirit *not* of God seeking to inflate our ego and diminish our reliance on God.

One of the most powerful words I learned from Jinny Ditzler was *abundance*. Of course, I had heard this word before, but I never realized how much the idea of scarcity drove me to desolate places of fear that, in turn, led to unhealthy behaviors. If we understand there is abundance in the world, that God has provided all that we need, our fears are abolished. Abundance does not mean I have more than anyone else or even more than I have right now. It means I have enough. I have plenty.

We get the life of the voice we follow. Jesus said, "I came that they may have life, and have it abundantly" (John 10:10). That is the consolation we seek. This is not the same as "I have come to make them wealthy beyond their wildest dreams!" The paradox of financial wealth is that so many wealthy people are desolate, and so many people who suffer in poverty know God intimately. Interestingly, Ignatius says clearly in the First Principle and Foundation to seek neither wealth nor poverty but only to do the will of God. The tools of this life are used and sought only insofar as they bring us closer to God and are avoided if they distract us from God. Money is one of these tools. Money is not a reflection of your identity or God's. It is simply an instrument, and God calls each of us to use our resources in ways consistent with our spiritual path.

Ignatius warned that the desire for riches leads to thinking we are worthy of honor (the kind of honor and praise society gives those who drive expensive cars, wear designer clothes, and live in mansions). This, in turn, leads to our ego flying off the charts and our feeling a false sense of importance. This thinking is completely opposite of the will of God. People who think they are the greatest are often the most shallow, unable to acknowledge with humility all the gifts and conditions that made their success possible, including reliance on a Higher Power. Honor itself can be a challenge, even without riches. After all, is it wrong to desire the highest grade in the class if there is some reward linked to that grade? Why run a race if we don't want to win it? Competition and honor are huge motivators for achieving our desired goals. Like money, they are not bad in and of themselves—*if* they are seen as instruments of growth rather than the end game.

Big Things in Little Places

Many people think God's call is about a grandiose feat of faith or giving up everything you own (although that was a directive to the rich young man of the Gospels, so don't discount it too fast!). The truth is that often God calls us to be exactly where we are, serving those around us. One of my former colleagues was a brilliant technology guru who happened to be blind. Every day he went above and beyond in his work to teach people who are blind and visually impaired how to use computers and smartphones. Every day he changed lives and opened the world for people who would be completely marginalized without the skills he taught. And yet, he often talked to me about wishing he could go abroad so he could "really help people." He couldn't imagine God was using him exactly where he was. That was obviously a temptation of the spirit *not* of God to discount and belittle the goodness he was spreading.

Albert D'Souza, SJ, is quoted as saying, "For a long time, it had seemed to me that life was about to begin—real life. But there was always some obstacle in the way, something to be got through first, some unfinished business, time still to be served, a debt to be paid. Then life would begin. At last, it dawned on me that these obstacles were my life."[36]

Sometimes discerning your spiritual path offers you an opportunity to go outside your comfort zone, maybe way outside to a different part of the world or a different job. Other times it may mean considering in a new way what you are doing right now as a call to serve exactly where you are. Either way, the call is about serving something greater than yourself.

Facing Obstacles

Sometimes, we dream of escaping reality, but that is not what we are doing here. In some of the relationships you have prioritized there are likely some challenging obstacles lying on your spiritual path—some emotional, some physical, some mental, some systemic. Imagining your coming year gives you a chance to sit with your reality and ask God to enlighten you, first, to understand what is possible, perhaps even the best-case scenario, and second, how you are called to act within it. These so-called obstacles are often our best teachers.

In the Gospel when Peter says, "God forbid it [you be killed]" to Jesus, Jesus responds, "Get behind me, Satan!" (Matthew 16:22–23). In other words, Jesus labels Satan an obstacle. Do not think for a second that your obstacles aren't the work of the spirit *not* of God! In fact, my spiritual director would tell me the more you are on track to connect with God, the harder the spirit *not* of God will work to block your path. "Get behind me" is another way of saying, "Follow me," or "Co-labor with me," or "Don't block me."

One fellow pilgrim shared that when he completed this part of the process, the only thing he could imagine was hugging his brother with whom he had had a falling out years earlier. It was very odd, but he couldn't imagine doing anything else with him—not getting a cup of coffee or taking a walk or even the conversations they would have in order to get to that point. His imagination was so fixated on hugging and being hugged by his brother that he could almost feel it. He knew what his brother was wearing, how tall his brother was, and how his eyes welled up. This was the state of being he had to be in to reach his goal.

What Is Already on the Horizon

While you are imagining the coming year, know that this isn't just wishful thinking. This prayerful time offers you a chance to prepare for any coming realities in light of your new Sacred Mantra and who you are called to be. For me, like it or not, my daughter will graduate from high school and go off to college. As much as I might want to, I can't make time stand still. What we bring to imaginative prayer is the context and reality within which we live, and we ask for the courage to change what we can and to accept what we cannot change. With each relationship begin with what is a given on the horizon. Imagine yourself—at your best—walking through it.

You Do You!

Remember: you only control yourself! A dream that someone with whom you have had a falling out will come to you to apologize is not within your control. We pray ardent petitions to God for safety, freedom from distress, and relief from burdens. However, God cannot grant us the relief that must come from the hearts and actions of others. We can only control our responses to the actions of others. In your imagining with God of how you will *be* in each relationship, identify your part of the dance. The other may choose to follow or stop dancing. That is on them. It is on you to free yourself.

The Serenity Prayer of Reinhold Niebuhr offers a beautiful way to identify your part of the dance: "Lord, grant me the serenity to accept the things I cannot change, the courage to change the things I can, and the wisdom to know the difference." This prayer helps us to discern and recognize the Spirit of God from the spirit *not* of God.

The best way to modify the behaviors of others is to change our own behaviors that may contribute to the dance of toxicity in a relationship. To be a victim of another person's behavior is toxic to your own soul. Others will choose their world view and behaviors. You are called to choose yours within that reality.

Time to Imagine with Your Walking Partner

Edward Kinerk, SJ, implores, "We need to dream if we are to stay spiritually and apostolically alive."[37] Be open to what might be possible if you and your Walking Partner stay intimately connected on this journey. Be aware of any resistance inside of you and gently tell that voice that you are not to be bothered right now because you are dreaming, imagining, and considering what might be possible.

Use your Ignatian imagination to put yourself in that state of being your heart is desiring. Describe it in feeling, form, and function. What is going on? What are the colors? Smells? Sounds? Who is there? What does it feel like? How do you see the others involved? Some people prefer to draw their imagined states of being before putting them into words.

The questions below are prompts for your imaginative prayer. Consider how you might answer them for each of your priority relationships.

Ask yourself and your Walking Partner:

- What would the next highest rating for this relationship look like?
- How am I called to *be* in this relationship, given my capacities and drivers?
- What do I imagine the other person in this relationship most needs from me?
- I feel most whole in this relationship when . . .
- I have always dreamed of . . .
- What can I manifest over the course of the coming months or year?

Start with the relationship you identified as your Greatest Invitation for Growth and describe your heart's desires for that relationship. Don't let the spirit *not* of God stop you from putting anything down. You will judge and discern your goals in the next chapter. Savor this opportunity to imagine what is possible with God.

Colloquy 26: Imagining What Is Possible with God

Write the valiant name you have given to each of your eight priority relationships from Colloquy 22a. Then, starting with your Greatest Invitation for Growth, take time to sit with your Walking Partner and imagine what you are being called to in each relationship over the coming months.

Relationship 1

I imagine . . .

Relationship 2

I imagine . . .

Relationship 3

I imagine . . .

Relationship 4

I imagine . . .

Relationship 5

I imagine . . .

Relationship 6

I imagine . . .

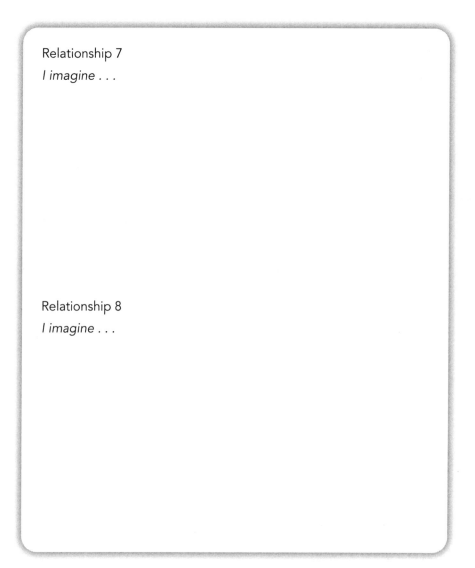

Relationship 7
I imagine . . .

Relationship 8
I imagine . . .

One fellow pilgrim reflected that grappling with this question illustrated how we can grow in so many ways once we see how things really are and what's most important in our life. Consolation feels like a giant *yes!* If these dreams reflect the deepest healthy desires of your heart, they will in some way praise, reverence, and serve God by allowing you to be fully you, a reflection of the divine within you. Trust that *yes!*

Chapter 10

What Is on the Horizon of My Spiritual Path?

Setting Your Spiritual Path Goals

> *"I'm going on an adventure!"*
>
> Bilbo Baggins

Once you have some idea of what the coming year might entail, you actualize this vision with concrete tasks and outcomes. It is finally time to set goals for each of your relationships. Ultimately, we live out our relationship with God through our relationships with others and ourselves. This living out requires action. Our response to the recognition of the love in our lives (affirmed in your Sacred Mantra) is our action in this world. In the Gospel story of feeding the five thousand, Jesus, in essence, tells the disciples that it is up to them to feed the hungry (see Matthew 14:16). Jesus again reiterates that faith is about action when he says, "For I was hungry and you gave me food, I was thirsty and you gave me something to drink, I was a stranger and you welcomed me, I was naked and you gave me clothing, I was sick and you took care of me, I was in prison and you visited me" (Matthew 25:35–36). Pope Francis reminds us of this calling, saying, "We should actively and creatively seek to deepen our desires and to make them more concrete."[38]

Goals achieved are states of being. They come in moments in our lives, often fleeting moments, just like those moments of consolation we talked about earlier. I think they come in fleeting moments because they are times when we step closer to our Godliness, an experience that is so powerful our frail humanity can handle only a moment of it at a time. But even in those fleeting moments, there is a bittersweet recognition that it is all about the journey. In the day-to-day of walking our spiritual path, so many unexpected consolations offer greater consolation than achieving the end goal. These include the consolations of becoming, trusting, gratitude, a new state of being, and a life we never could have imagined.

Often when we reach one state of being, we experience the longing for yet another, different state of being. That is growth. I want *to be* a mom turns into I want *to be* a more patient mom. By articulating goals that reflect where we feel called and who we are called to be, we take a huge step into that vision. The difference between goal setting and wishful thinking is your active participation as the co-laborer to reach the desired state of being. The moments we feel the most whole are those when we align with the Spirit of God's desires for us, that is, when we *are being* who God has called us to be. Again, Edward Kinerk, SJ, reaffirms this by saying, "The timid soul who first breaks down the blockage of fear and puts authentic desires into action will find not only a deeper assimilation to Christ but also the exhilaration which active courage provides for ever new desires and deeds."[39]

Your goals are a succinct articulation of that state of being you are imagining. They are the horizon toward which we move. Your spiritual path consists of all the actions you take to get to that horizon. You can't just magically snap your fingers and arrive at your destination, but you can actively work toward it. Being precise in articulating a goal will make a difference in how likely you are to attain what you desire. This chapter offers some practical insights on how to write them.

Two Types of Goals

Process goals establish a habitual way of acting. For example, I share breakfast with my husband three times a week. Process goals require setting aside time for repetitive actions. By the end of your plan, you want this to be a way of life for you because you trust or imagine that the activity itself will bring you consolation. It takes time to work up to process goals and make them stick. The challenge with process goals is to be sure they achieve the desired effect. I can have breakfast with my husband, but if we are both on our phones the whole time, that will likely not bring me the desired effect. Fellow *Best Year Yet!* coach Kris Gleason suggests that for process goals like working out three times a week we add the phrase "so that . . ." Thus, "I will work out three times a week so that I can play soccer with my grandson for twenty minutes straight." This way, we are clear about what ultimate outcome or state of being we are seeking. Without a defined outcome, process goals can feel like drudgery. Finally, many people jump into a process goal with a burst of energy at the beginning without giving themselves time to build up to a full habitual level, so don't expect to start where you seek to end.

Outcome goals culminate in a new state of being. However, rather than doing repetitive actions, we take multiple steps—and perhaps even unknown actions—over the course of our pilgrimage. The challenge of outcome goals is the ongoing attention required to be sure we don't procrastinate in taking necessary steps to the end of the allotted time. A helpful way to create an outcome goal is to finish this sentence: *A year from now I want to be able to say that I . . .* Outcome goals should remind us of what we imagined and the consolation those visions brought.

Here are examples of the two ways to write a goal.

Process goal: Exercise three times a week for an hour each time so that I prevent diabetes. **Outcome** goal: Weigh twenty-five pounds less by this time next year so that I prevent diabetes.

Process goal: Learn how to cook a new vegetarian meal each week so that I have variety in my diet. **Outcome** goal: Have a repertoire of at least fourteen new vegetarian meals that I can cook by the end of the year so that I have variety in my diet.

For now, write out either form of a goal and discern later which is the most motivational for you. Best practices suggest that having a mix of both outcome and process goals on your Spiritual Path helps you to grow the most. Here are some sample goals from my journey reflecting a relationship vision for you to consider.

My Journey

Personal Coach: Spend one hour a day for five days a week on Spanish so in one year I can have a basic conversation in Spanish and understand the majority of what I hear.

Parent: Spend half a day each month with Joe and Lucy doing what they want so we make memories and get to know one another better.

Daughter: Transition dad to independent living and sell the house in a way that honors his priorities.

A Note about Feelings

As odd as it may sound, a feeling isn't a state of being you can work toward. Put another way, our goal isn't a feeling. This whole exercise is about setting yourself up for *experiencing* consolation, which is movement toward God. Unfortunately, there is no algorithm that guarantees that state of being. We can work all year toward a goal and not feel the way we expect to feel when we get there. There are different schools of thought on how well we can control our feelings, but in general, feelings arise, and the more we are present to them and acknowledge them, the more we are able to understand where they are coming from and choose how they influence our actions, tone, words, and behaviors. More important, Ignatius suggests we observe those feelings and discern which Spirit is giving rise to them. The ultimate goal then is the context that you are seeking to put yourself in so that you experience consolation. Rather than have a goal of being happy or more confident, articulate a goal that reflects the situation or state of being to which you are being called. When you get to that desired state of being (and along the way), then you can discern whether you actually feel more whole, more complete, more integrated with the desires of your heart. For example, the goal "Be happy in my job" would have you trying to orchestrate a feeling, where "Be in a job that utilizes my strengths" has clear direction for you to orchestrate a situation that is likely to give you consolation. Consolation comes from God alone. It is a grace. The best you can do is align your identity, including your Sacred Mantra, values, and strengths, with your goals and attune your heart through noticing, listening, and prayer to the interior movements along the way.

Wordsmithing Your Goals

How you articulate your goals makes a significant impact on your ability to accomplish them. In those human moments of weakness, when that spirit *not* of God is working against you walking the spiritual path, you will look for the loopholes in your goals to convince yourself you are fulfilling them. Your heart may be telling you something different. Clarity about our goals motivates us to work toward them and have something definitive to celebrate when we reach that place we are called to be.

Begin by writing your goals to be SMART. This acronym was first coined by George Doran in 1981 and holds true even today.[40]

Specific: Goals need to define a clear result. Does your goal answer who, what, where, when, and why? The "how" will likely come in the tactics you outline later as part of your monthly, ongoing review. It's okay to not know exactly how you will reach a goal at this point. Part of your journey will be to figure that out.

Measurable: Finding some way to measure a goal lets you know when you have achieved it for sure. The focus here should be on how much or how many; feelings aren't measurable. Love is not measurable. But you can set indicators for yourself that reflect what you are trying to express. Would others agree that those indicators are an adequate reflection?

Attainable: Is there at least an 80 percent chance of success? Read that again. Is there, given your dedicated attention, an 80 percent chance that you can reach this goal? Why 80 percent? Because life happens even to the best of us. But if when starting out you don't have a fighting chance to reach a particular goal, then you are wasting your time. (Note: there is not an 80 percent chance you will win the lottery!) Be honest about the odds of life. Also be aware of whether you have let yourself off the hook and set a goal that is too easy. Is it 100 percent attainable—a guarantee with minimal effort on your part? If it is just a repeat of what you are already doing, then you likely need to push yourself out of your comfort zone to seek that growth to which you are being called.

Relevant: Relevant means that the goal is important to the people you serve, and to your future viability, and is consistent with your vision and values. Is this goal what your heart desires? Is it relevant to your calling? You may feel called to work for justice for the poor, in which case attending law school would be understandably relevant, but studying astronomy might not be relevant. There is nothing wrong with studying astronomy, but making this choice means you are seeking a different heart's desire.

Timebound: This is a six-month or one-year plan. That is significant both in the long and short term. In the short term, you are setting monthly steps to reach this goal by the end of your plan. If there are only two steps to go and you can reach this goal in three months, do you have other goals that will keep calling you to grow for the rest of the year? Are there follow-up activities or next steps you should include to be sure you get the full benefit of your goal? At the other end of the time spectrum, this is only a year or six months. Rome was not built in a day. Don't be afraid to dream big and use this plan's goal as a stepping stone and assessment point for part of your multi-year journey. A freshman going into college obviously wants to graduate, but the one-year goal is to successfully complete the first year.

The Spiritual Path process contains an addendum to the SMART goal acronym to be sure that your goals reflect not just what you want to accomplish but also your mindset going into this journey. Your goals need to also be SASSY.

Spirit-driven: This is a reminder that you are co-laboring here. Allow some time and space for your Walking Partner to speak into your goals. God is not only inviting you into these goals; God can multiply their impact beyond your wildest dreams. Some might call it the ripple effect. Imagine what difference achieving this goal might mean beyond the relationship at hand. The Spirit enables exponential impact.

Accountable: Do you want to be held accountable for this goal? Are you ready to accept this responsibility? Do you accept this invitation willingly? Yes, you will face challenges that get in the way and days when you don't want to put in the effort. Is this a goal that you will be able to say, "The buck stops with me," or "I can make this happen"? Accountability also means the goal does not require you to change other people. I can't ensure my son gets straight As, but I can ensure I am available every night to review my son's homework.

Shareable: Are you willing to share this goal with others? The moment you share a goal with other people it becomes more than just yours, and it takes flight. You don't have to broadcast it to the world, but at least be willing to articulate it with someone—your spiritual director, your spouse, a member of your family. Just to speak your desires to another human being means that you are taking them seriously. Sharing your calling and confidence in God being a part of your goal can inspire others to their own goals. Ignatius counseled that there is a reason we sometimes want to keep things in the dark. The spirit *not* of God doesn't want to be seen or brought into the light. If your goal is something you aren't willing to share, maybe it is coming from a place other than the Spirit of God.

Start now! Is this goal one that you are ready to jump into? Procrastination is not a consequence of consolation or movement closer to God. If you were given the gift of ten free hours tomorrow, would you dive into this goal? Saying you have a goal but you will start working toward it in a few months is often a recipe for failure. Can you say that one month from today you will have made some measurable progress toward this goal?

Yes! When you imagine reaching this goal, do you have a sense of consolation? Would achieving the goal make your spirit just want to shout *yes!*? There are no halfhearted desires on the spiritual path. You must be willing to do whatever it takes to achieve them; you must be wholehearted!

These parameters are meant to help you make your goals concrete and actionable. Your confidence grows when you are clear on what you are being called to do. Resist the temptation to strive to write the perfect goal, which may lead to anxiety. If it isn't perfectly SMART and SASSY the first time you write it, that's fine. Better to get it on paper and go back later and wordsmith it to meet the criteria.

No one is saying it will be easy. Yet there is no need to make it unnecessarily difficult. More important, no one is saying you alone will make these goals happen. In fact, no one ever walks their spiritual path alone. There is a Power beyond anything you can imagine walking with you every step of the way, and there are others waiting out there to journey with you.

And with that preparation, we begin the Cycle of Growth again.

Brainstorming Goals for Each Relationship

For each of the relationships you identified and named in chapter 8, brainstorm a few different goals that reflect what you imagined in chapter 9. This is just brainstorming, so write whatever comes to mind, and be as creative as you want. Sometimes the seed of a goal is the most important part. You have no commitment to any of these goals yet. This is called green-light thinking, which means you completely ignore the red-light voice that is saying to you, *There is no way I can do that! This is going to be too hard. People will laugh at me. I have never done this before. What makes me think I can do it now?* And on and on goes the spirit *not* of God. Green light means go. What might it look like if you weren't afraid of this? Write the desires of your heart on paper as possible goals. You can wordsmith and discern among them later. For now, put down what some goals for each relationship *might* be. Include not only new activities but also ongoing activities that reflect your current relationships and that you might take to a new level. Finally, let your Walking Partner surprise you! If you go into this thinking that you already know the outcome, how open are you to the invitation to grow? Ignatius taught, "Everything has the potential to draw forth from me a fuller love and life. Yet my desires are often fixed, caught on illusions of fulfillment. I ask that God, through my freedom, may orchestrate my desires in a vibrant, loving melody rich in harmony."[41] Prayerfully brainstorm at least two *possible* goals for each relationship. Start with the relationship you identified as your Greatest Invitation for Growth, and brainstorm at least three potential goals for that one relationship.

Colloquy 27: Goal Brainstorming

Starting with your Greatest Invitation for Growth, enter the valiant name for each of your priority relationships in the blank. Then brainstorm two or more possible goals for each relationship. Be sure to invite your Walking Partner to brainstorm with you.

Valiant Relationship Name _____
(Greatest Invitation for Growth) and Possible Goals:

Valiant Relationship Name _____
and Possible Goals:

Valiant Relationship Name _____
and Possible Goals:

Valiant Relationship Name _____
and Possible Goals:

Valiant Relationship Name _____
and Possible Goals:

Valiant Relationship Name _____
and Possible Goals:

Valiant Relationship Name _____
and Possible Goals:

Valiant Relationship Name _____
and Possible Goals:

Valiant Relationship Name _____
and Possible Goals:

When you have brainstormed the goals that best reflect your vision for each relationship, take a step back and review the list in its entirety. Observe your inner voice as you feel either energy or trepidation at any goal. Ask your Walking Partner for the grace to understand where that feeling is coming from. Ask if there are other potential opportunities you missed.

Judge: Discerning Your Spiritual Path Goals

At this point you have brainstormed multiple potential goals for each relationship. You have multiple ways for walking your spiritual path and becoming closer to God by growing into that person you are called to be. Now comes the discernment. Which of these goals will you embrace for the coming year? Which invitations will you accept?

Ignatius describes three ways of making an election or decision. A decision is discerned when we admit honestly what is moving inside us, when we know the desires of our heart, and when we identify which spirit these desires reflect. That spirit *not* of God is present in our doubts about our calling as well as in our enjoyment of distractions and temptations that move us away from our calling. If identifying your goals is difficult, don't hesitate to work with a spiritual director, just as you would talk with a doctor about physical ailments. Ignatius gives us the Rules of Discernment to aid in this process. For now, work through the process on your own, and confirm your discernment with your spiritual director, a trusted friend, or fellow pilgrim afterward.

In the first circumstance for making a decision, according to Ignatius, you have no doubt, and the right decision is unmistakably clear. In these circumstances, the opportunity makes your soul leap, hits you like a lightning bolt or a blast of air, and wakes you up. It is obvious that this is the right thing to do. You may not know all the details, or how this decision will play out, or its full implications, but your heart shouts a giant *yes! This is the right thing to do.* If you have any goals on your list that just leap out at you screaming, "Pick me! Pick me!" you might as well pick them, because they aren't going away. They will likely still be there next year and beyond, nagging at you if you don't choose them now.

In the second circumstance for making a decision, you feel unsettled, because the decision does not emerge as an obvious path to moving closer to God or more fully toward your calling. Hold this tension gently and reflect on the consolation or desolation that stirs in you as you do so. As you consider a goal, does it leave you with more hope or with more anxiety? Hesitation and agitation are very different feelings. In this circumstance, one Ignatian practice is to ponder various alternatives. For example, spend three days imagining that you are determined to go down one path. Share that path with others. Go through your day behaving in ways it would require to be all-in on that path. Then, repeat the same process for the other path. After both paths have been tested, reflect back over how your spirit felt during each of those three days. When were you lighter and more yourself? Conversely, when was your spirit more burdened and anxious? You may not need six full days to discern your goals for next year right now. If following this Spiritual Path process brings you to a major life decision, like marriage or a vocational direction, take more time to be fully aware of your true and deepest heart's desire. For most of us, though, our annual goals will call us more to changes in attitude and daily activity than to a complete life refocus. Your annual goal may be to spend this year exploring that potential calling so that by the end of the year or by some point within the year you have clearly made a discernment. Additionally, Ignatius suggests asking yourself what you would advise a friend in your situation. Or imagine you are lying on your deathbed and looking back on this moment. What can you imagine advising your younger self? You might not always feel a leap of *yes* if you know that the journey to get there is going to be tough, but is there a leap of *yes* when you imagine sitting in this room a year from now and you can say you reached that goal? All of these imaginative prayers allow you to sit with your potential goals and your Walking Partner and discern what you want to do with your time. Have a good conversation about them.

In the third circumstance for making a decision, your emotions are calm. In this circumstance, Ignatius says to analyze your choices logically, pros and cons, and see where choosing a goal might lead you. You may need more information than you have at this point. You may need time to experience one choice over another. In this situation, you are trusting two things: your freedom to change direction down the road (thus, this is not the method to use for discerning a lifelong commitment), and the certainty that God will continue to work through and within you in such a way that the rightness of the choice will be revealed.

Keep these three methods of making a decision in mind as you narrow down the goals worthy of your commitment. Mark Thibodeaux, SJ, a spiritual director to Jesuits in formation and author of many books including *God's Voice Within*, cautions us to be wary that we aren't called to every holy action! You may not be the best person for this goal, or this may not be the right time to try to reach this goal, or it may be the right goal but the wrong method.[42]

There is significant debate over how many goals is too many. This is a less-is-more situation. On any spiritual path, being present to the moment at hand is vital. In this case, how present can you be in each moment of your day to be intentional about why you are there and what action you are taking? Some experts advise no more than ten goals. Others advise no more than three. While you have narrowed down your top eight relationships, choosing one goal for each would still set a very high bar for the year. Trying to grow so much in one year can lead to desolation rather than consolation. Be honest with yourself. Some people are fine with three or five, especially while they adjust to having a written Spiritual Path to review each month. You *must* choose at least one goal—maybe more than one—as your personal caretaker. You can choose more than one goal for any relationship, particularly for your Greatest Invitation for Growth. You also are free to not choose any goals from one of your relationships, as long as you recognize and consent to the relationship not being a priority on your plan. You are not ending that relationship; rather, you are prioritizing and focusing on the invitations that are being offered in other areas of your life. Try very hard not to avoid a potential relationship goal you are being called to grow through. Again, Edward Kinerk, SJ, encourages, "We should not be afraid of our desires. This may sound strange, but we ought not be too hasty in assuming that the contrary is true. Authentic desires nearly always involve some risk."[43]

Wilke Au and Noreen Cannon Au offer a great spectrum for distinguishing between the affective states that our potential goals elicit in us.[44]

- **Wishing something will happen** is not rooted in reality but in magic or something beyond the person.
- **Instinctual desire** is based on our current feelings (like something that makes me happy), which are fleeting and lack ongoing commitment.
- **Tentative desires** are desires with reservations, as in "I would like that, but . . . [insert hesitation here]."
- **Definitive desires** show up in how we allocate our time, money, and other resources, as well as in our actual behavior choices, and are expressed as "I want . . ." The definitive desire to walk more intentionally with our Walking Partner in each priority relationship is what we are seeking here.

Finally, when we discern among possible goals for these relationships, keep in mind the Ignatian spiritual practice of seeking *magis*. *Magis* is the Latin word for *more* or *greater*. Ignatius implored those doing the Spiritual Exercises to always push the boundaries of their comfort zone, to be willing to do more to get closer to God. However, in our twenty-first-century culture, the idea of more is far too often associated with quantity—as in more money, more time, more busy work, more stuff—all of which leaves us feeling exhausted and in desolation. In the context of Ignatian spirituality, however, *magis* is the practice of going deeper into a relationship, not settling for superficiality. We need to always be open to and seek a greater capacity to love. Practicing *magis* does not mean we are motivated by guilt, but rather that we desire to better know Christ. We try to free ourselves from fearful thinking that *more* or *deeper* isn't possible.

You began this process open to what the Spiritual Path questions might bring and how you might envision the future as the person you are called and created to be. These goals that you have brainstormed are your possible responses. Take a few minutes to sit with them, pray for guidance, and discern which goals you are called to. Ask your Walking Partner which is the best path. Be open to challenges. Be aware of consolation or desolation as you go through this process. Does naming a goal and imagining reaching it energize you? Does it feel like a response to grace? Or maybe a *yes* that says, *I know this won't be easy, but it will help me to grow closer to what God created me to be.*

Prayer for Discerning Goals

Lord, Spirit of Wisdom,
you have given me the coming days of my life. For all you have given me, I now seek to give them back to you and be in your service through my strengths and capacities. I believe these are the healthy desires you have placed in my heart to bring me closer to knowing you. I am committed to walking with you. Give me your insight to know what directions to take. Give me your courage to walk those paths that are challenging or countercultural. Release me from any desires that are not healthy for me and for those around me. Help me to trust that you are in these invitations for me to grow.

On the previous brainstorm list (Colloquy 27), circle the three to ten goals you are called to in the coming year. At least one or more goals must be from your Greatest Invitation for Growth and your personal caretaker. Wordsmith them to be sure they are SMART and SASSY; then write them in the next colloquy. You may want to share them with others to help you shape and speak into them.

Colloquy 28: My Spiritual Path Goals

After discerning the goals to which you are being called, wordsmith them to meet the SMART and SASSY criteria and write them here starting with the goal(s) for your Greatest Invitation for Growth.

1.

2.

3.

4.

5.

6.

7.

8.

9.

10.

One Last Review

Look back at the values and strengths you identified as your Sources of Energy. Do your goals resonate with those? Do any of them conflict with your values or strengths? One participant in a workshop noted simplicity as one of her three values, but when her plan had ten disparate goals, her first thought was how her plan itself didn't seem to reflect that value. She dropped three of her potential goals and felt she was being true to her values. Is each goal worded in a way that will pass the SMART and SASSY test? Are they exciting or hopeful to you? Wordsmith them if you need to.

When you clarify your goals, consider them in their totality. Is there still an 80 percent chance of success for each goal, given the time and energy you will put into your other goals? Do you see these relationships growing in their reflection of God's presence, or is it going to be hard to grow in one area if you focus on another as well? Adjust your goals as necessary, even if it means dropping one completely. Again, dropping a goal doesn't mean you are dropping that relationship. It means that relationship will continue to function as it was before. The only goals you cannot drop are those advancing your Greatest Invitation for Growth and your personal caretaker relationship.

Add one more consideration to your discernment. Be gentle with yourself. What difference would it make if your Walking Partner were whispering, *Dude, you can't fail!* In all honesty, if your ultimate goal is to move closer to God, to better reflect the love of God, and to be more fully your truest self, the goals you choose today represent your attempt to get there. As Thomas Merton, the American Trappist monk, poet, writer, mystic, social activist, and theologian put it, "I believe that the desire to please You does in fact please You."[45] No matter what goals you choose or don't choose, you are loved beyond measure. Finalize your goals in the light of that freedom.

Act: Writing Your Goals

When you are ready, write your goals on your Spiritual Path plan at the back of the book. As you write them, imagine you are writing your personal scripture. You are writing the ways God will be manifested in this world through you in the coming months. Writing them on your Spiritual Path is your sacramental act of commitment to them.

Your goals offer you a page of consolation, a road map toward growth in your capacity to reflect the divine within you. This is your mountaintop moment where you and your Walking Partner are looking over the valley of the months before you.

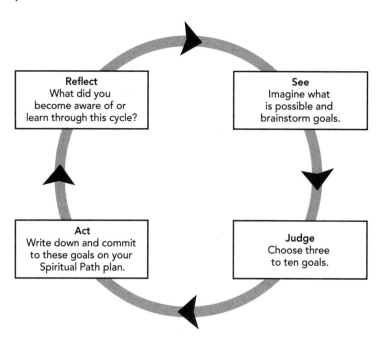

Reflect

This plan created by you and your Walking Partner is a great grace! Reflect now on what stirred inside you through this process and looking forward, knowing the journey is just beginning.

Colloquy 29: Reflections on the Experience of Discerning My Goals

What moved in me throughout this Cycle of Growth by setting my goals? What did I learn?

My Walking Partner's response to discerning these goals with me:

Remember, the ultimate horizon of this Spiritual Path is the Principle and Foundation, which is to praise, reverence, and serve God, and in so doing to save your soul.

Each of the scenic overlooks in this journey have come at the points where you completed a full Cycle of Growth and wrote your own "sacred scripture," so to speak, that is, your personal writings on your Spiritual Path plan. We have already enjoyed the view at the first four scenic overlooks:

- articulating lessons to make your spiritual journey smoother;
- creating a Sacred Mantra, a faithful internal compass;
- identifying your unique Sources of Energy for this journey;
- discerning your goals and completing a one-page Spiritual Path plan.

But now we have come to the final leg of the journey:

- committing to the first steps on that path over the coming month and the tools you will use to stay on it.

Of course, you know that it is only after these next few chapters that the real journey begins.

PART 3

WALKING YOUR SPIRITUAL PATH

Chapter 11

How Do I Stay on My Spiritual Path?

Supportive Tools and Tips

We shape our tools and then our tools shape us.
JOHN CULKIN, SJ

My brother is the king of pre-trip planning. He once sent me a list of twenty-five items I would need for an easy hike. My idea of hiking gear includes a water bottle and decent shoes. His, on the other hand, included everything from bear spray to rain gear to carbohydrate bars. I complained about wanting to be free and not have to carry so much. He reassured me that everything on the list was meant to free me from pain along the way. Apparently, he expected me to trust experienced hikers who knew what they were doing! All the tools on his list were there for a good reason, based on his experience.

Walking a spiritual path and intentionally achieving your goals as a co-laborer with your Walking Partner is much the same. Experienced pilgrims will tell you that some tools are simply basic to this spiritual journey. These tools not only keep you motivated but also keep you safe and allow you to venture into the unknown with confidence.

Tool 1: Breathe

You have been given the gift of a lifetime. God's gift. As the poem by Linda Ellis says, it is the dash on your tombstone between your birthdate and your death date: *What matters is how we live and love and how we spend our dash.* Please don't waste the most precious gift of all: TIME. Manage your time instead of letting time manage you.

Time management is the biggest barrier for most people to walk their spiritual path. Many of us feel we don't have a minute for ourselves, let alone time to serve Something Greater than ourselves. So first, *breathe*. The easiest time management tool is to breathe and be present in the now. When you breathe, anxieties concerning the future lose their hold on you. Right here and now you are just fine. Focusing on breathing puts you in the See phase.

Recall Richard Rohr's understanding of *Yah-weh* being the sound of an inhale and an exhale. Trust that the Power of Infinite Love and Creativity is within each breath you take.

Tool 2: Practice God-Time Management

The Spiritual Path adapts Steven Covey's Time Management Matrix system into God-Time Management to help analyze how people use or waste time.[46] As a co-laborer with the Power of Infinite Love, the question is how you use your God-given time. This system can be used to reflect and learn when looking back, as well as to plan and prioritize when looking forward. Consider each task you do in light of being Required or Invited, Engaged or Disengaged.

- A **Required** task *must* be done, either because of an outside deadline or daily functioning and responsibilities.
- An **Invited** task is one that doesn't need to be done at this time; rather, it is there for you to do, and you choose to make the task a priority. Sometimes Invited tasks become Required tasks when we procrastinate too long or when there is a limited window of opportunity or a looming deadline.
- An **Engaged** task is one with a clear focus or purpose for your body, mind, or spirit.
- A **Disengaged** task asks only that we show up and go through the motions.

Each task you do during the day will fall into one of the four categories below, noting both the column and the row, and moving counterclockwise around the squares:

I. Required and Engaged

II. Required and Disengaged

III. Invited and Disengaged

IV. Invited and Engaged (God-Time)

God-Time Management	Required (Urgent)	Invited (Not Required)
Engaged **(Purposeful, Focused, Intentional)**	*I. Required and Engaged* Crises and emergencies Pressing problems Deadline-driven projects Important meetings Regular reporting	*IV. Invited and Engaged* Spiritual Path plan work Relationship enrichment Personal development Personal caretaking
Disengaged **(Distracted)**	*II. Required and Disengaged* Interruptions Meetings Other people's agendas New e-mails Habitual non-growth-filled activities	*III. Invited and Disengaged* Surfing the net Checking the inbox Binge-watching TV Participating in idle chatter

Too often we spend our days in the Required and Engaged category, putting out fires and addressing problems. This is the corner of true emergencies, but also of taxes and reporting requirements and projects with a deadline that aren't on your Spiritual Path. We all have these types of activities on our daily calendar that focus our attention on what needs to be done. This is the temptation of the good corner. These activities are really important; that is, they have a clear focus or purpose, given the many causes out there, but we prioritize them over our own goals either because of their seeming urgency or because of the guilt they inspire.

The Required and Disengaged activities are definitely distractions from what you claim is important to you. *Hurry! Hurry! Hurry! The Sale Ends Friday!* Or the habitual need to check that e-mail box every twenty minutes. These are the *shoulds* on our to-do lists, but in this category, discern whether they are truly required or if you feel that way because they are urgent to someone else, or if they could be accomplished more efficiently. Make a mental note when you notice that you are disengaged in a task and just a body in the room.

The Invited and Disengaged tasks are the biggest wasters of your lifetime. You aren't even getting brownie points in terms of helping others on their projects or agendas. These are the things we do to zone out, and for most Americans, they add up to over thirty-five hours a week![47] That's more than five hours a day of wasted lifetime. Anything in this category is sheer temptation from the spirit *not* of God. Do we all do these things? Yes. But they are addicting and numbing. God is never calling you to a numb or disengaged life.

Finally, consider those activities that fit into the upper-right-hand corner, Invited and Engaged. All too often these are what our heart desires to spend our lifetime doing, but the other squares somehow come first. This is the corner that holds your Spiritual Path activities. You have discerned they are important, but you do them as an invitation rather than as a requirement. If you are feeling something is a should, you are more likely to fit it in the required column. Invited and Engaged is the square of God Time—the square of growth. It's about creating space to engage your attention—mind, body, and spirit—but these activities are not yet urgent or required and therefore are in danger of being missed or postponed. Reading this book and creating your Spiritual Path plan is all God Time!

The Ignatian addition to God-Time Management recognizes that God is present in all things, in all the moments of your day, in the required and engaged daily tasks, and in the required but disengaged never-ending meetings. The question is, How are *you* showing up in these moments? In what ways do you experience that Presence? Do you experience consolation in these minutes as the person you are created to be, your best self, reflecting the Power of Infinite Love? Or do you experience desolation and feel your soul wasting away from lack of attention? God's presence invites you to stop the life-numbing activities and affirms your desire to spend your time on something meaningful. The mystics among us can find and be present to God in most things, so they live in that upper-right-hand corner of Invited and Engaged much of the time. They recognize that less in life is required of us than we think. That is where we seek to live, in that *yes!* to the invitation to be more present to all our moments.

Fill out your own God-Time Management here for a typical day as a way of visualizing which quadrant most of your activities fall into now.

Colloquy 30: Completing a Current
God-Time Management Plan

God-Time Management	Required (Urgent)	Invited (Not Required)
Engaged (Purposeful, Focused, Intentional)	I.	IV.
Disengaged (Distracted)	II.	III.

Is your Walking Partner present to you in all of these? In what ways?

How to Get More God Time

Consider making the following practices part of your time-management tool kit while walking your spiritual path.

Schedule your Spiritual Path tasks first. I call this tool My Big God Rocks. The double meaning reminds me that my God is big, and the Spirit rocks my world, messages that are both very motivational to me. Perhaps you have seen the demonstration of trying to fit lots of things into a jar and then it becomes clear that the order in which they go in is the key to making everything fit. Our tendency is to spend our time first on the *Required/Engaged* activities (in the upper-left-hand corner and go counterclockwise to *Required/Disengaged* activities in the lower-left-hand corner). Then we tend toward the *Invited/Disengaged* time wasters (in the lower-right-hand corner) and leave the *Invited/Engaged* activities as a last priority. Using the God-Time Management strategy prioritizes the *Invited/Engaged* activities, including the tasks related to the goals on our Spiritual Path every day.

Typical Time Management Habits	Required (Urgent)	Invited (Not Required)
Engaged (Purposeful, Focused, Intentional)	First priority	Last priority
Disengaged (Distracted)	Second priority	Third priority

God-Time Management Habits	Required (Urgent)	Invited (Not Required)
Engaged (Purposeful, Focused, Intentional)	Second priority	First priority
Disengaged (Distracted)	Third priority	Last priority

My Journey

When my husband and I first joined the Ignatian Associates, our faith community, we committed to a time-consuming formation process: an hour of daily prayer, regular meetings with a spiritual director, and a weekly two-hour group formation meeting. I did not believe I could fit this all in while raising three kids. But honestly, it was easy to let go of so many other things I used to convince myself were necessary. That time was so good for me, so consoling. Twenty-plus years later I can see it was the most impactful period of my life.

There is a bit of a leap of faith in this strategy. We affirm that our heart's desires are legitimate and worthy of priority over the things the world requires of us. We believe we will still fulfill those requirements that are a part of being human. Over time, as we focus on the tasks that bring us consolation and avoid those that bring us desolation, we naturally move into this corner of the grid. That growth starts with scheduling the tasks we have discerned right now to be Invited and Engaged first.

On a weekly basis, review your Spiritual Path plan and identify your commitments in the coming week. Schedule those activities first. Literally, put them on your calendar. Block out time before you schedule even required, engaged activities. Don't worry. Those activities will get done around your availability. A good rule of thumb is to schedule at least three to five Spiritual Path tasks weekly. Daily practices like prayer or exercise are big steps each week even though you repeat them on multiple days. The earlier in the day you schedule your steps, the more likely you will be to get them done.

One good way to think about being a co-laborer of your life is to see what is on your calendar as your response to God. *You gave me this time, and here is what I am going to do with it this week.* I control my calendar when putting things on it, but once written, the calendar controls me to make it happen. It is a contract of sorts with my best self.

Minimize the Required boxes. Schedule and complete any tasks that require your attention and engagement before they become required or urgent, otherwise they become the focus of your day. This may mean making lunches the night before so the next morning you are free for that early run. Or take the initiative to schedule a meeting at a time that works for you rather than wait for an invitation at someone else's convenience. It also means drawing a hard line against what others say is required of you when it is their procrastination that requires your involvement at any given moment.

Discern your responsibility for the agendas or needs of other people. A fellow pilgrim commented that she spends 99 percent of her time managing the emotions of other people. As a full-time mother of young children, that may be part of her vocational work and a necessary component of how she walks her spiritual path. On the other hand, adults' emotions are theirs to manage. Other people may want you to feel that something is required of you, that you should be engaged simply because it is a priority to *them*. However, beware when their expectation leaves you feeling the urgency but not the sense of engagement. Be wary of the "should" monster here. If a task really does not engage you, why spend your *dash* on it? The discernment you need is whether you are *required* to do these activities or are *invited* to do them by virtue of your vocation or calling. Do you see those tasks as part of who you are called to be? If so, they offer easy moments of consolation even in the most mundane tasks. If not, recognize that this task is not part of your spiritual path. To understand it as someone else's agenda helps minimize the value attributed to it, and thus the claim on your time. Consider your Sacred Mantra. Discern if there are activities from the agendas of other people that you can drop from your routine to allow more time for the activities you desire to help you grow. It is good to say no to things you are not called to.

Prioritize self-care. Often people neglect self-care activities, thinking they are unnecessary or perceiving them as selfish. I have a friend who felt it was selfish to ask anything for herself in prayer! Ignatius himself struggled with getting this balance right; for years he neglected the activities of self-care to the point of near starvation. Those activities that refresh us and keep us healthy rather than disengaged and numb are very important because they are life giving. These activities always belong in the Engaged row where you intentionally honor your body, mind, and spirit.

Integrate Required/Engaged tasks with Spiritual Path tasks. Daily tasks such as cooking dinner and walking the dog can be integrated creatively with Spiritual Path tasks. Walking the dog was the way my husband and I ensured we spent quality time together. The dog didn't care if we both showed up, but *we* did. Think about *how* you do required activities in your life; create intention and build opportunities for growth into them.

Set a timer. Whether for prayer time, screen time, or any other activity, setting a timer allows you to be intentional about that time so other distractions take a back seat. Timers also help set intentional limits, so you move on to the next task without wasting the day. Setting schedules and a timer to manage the time spent on e-mail and the Internet frees you from constantly checking it and being distracted. If you spend significant time checking news feeds, e-mails, tweets, etc., you are looking for distraction, and consolation is not found in distraction. Consolation is found in those relationships you have prioritized in your life. Reaching your Spiritual Path goals requires that you be intentional.

Tool 3: The Daily *Examen*

Walking a spiritual path without daily prayer is like hiking a mountain without shoes. You can do it, but it's going to be a lot more painful, and it is more likely you will slip and fall and hurt yourself. The *examen* is your best tool for accountability and listening to the Spirit of God as you walk your spiritual path. A daily *examen*, an essential spiritual practice instituted by St. Ignatius himself, is an intimate conversation or colloquy with your Walking Partner conducted at the close of each day about how the journey went during that day. The *examen* can be seen as a mini-Cycle of Growth. You *see* your heart, thoughts, and actions over the past day as an outside observer. Within that seeing, you recognize movement toward or away from the Power of Infinite Love. This is not a mental checklist of what you did the day before and ensuring you checked boxes. Rather, it is an observation of how a task felt during, after, and in retrospect. In the *examen*, you ask God to give you the color commentary on your day. As you review the hours and activities, you might hear something like, *Do you recognize how good that made you feel? Do that again when you have the chance.* Or, *Why was that nagging in my gut all day? Is there something about how I was acting that isn't right for me?*

For a long time, I questioned and doubted the whole idea of being a writer, let alone writing a book. But in my daily *examen*, I noticed that the hours I sat at the keyboard flew by. My heart would leap at the insights I gained in the process of articulating something. Or the feeling of consolation I experienced in rereading what I wrote. I may not be a great spiritual writer, but through the consolation it brings me, I have learned it is worth my time, even if it only allows me and my relationship with the Power of Infinite Love to grow.

There are different ways to do the *examen*. Each method emphasizes the following steps:

- Begin with gratitude.
- Place yourself in God's presence.
- Affirm your freedom to be there.
- Let go of worries, fears, and to-do lists.
- Seek an awareness of what God wants to teach you.
- Review all you have done and felt over the previous time period.

An *examen* designed specifically for the Spiritual Path process is offered in the back of this book. (See page 215.)

One surefire way to stay on your spiritual path is to bring your God-Time categories to the *examen*. "In what corner did I spend my time yesterday? Did that activity bring me consolation or desolation?" Through the *examen* you can find unplanned tasks that filled your day. In this conversation, you learn the impact of each activity, and you reflect on how you either handled them or allowed them to handle you. In the spiritual journey of Ignatius, it was as he looked back that he saw with clarity how his daily experiences had affected his life and his spirituality. Even when a part of the *examen* proved difficult or painful, like admitting to sinfulness, he did it in the interest of growth and consolation. Much like physical exercise, this *examen* helps you see what has been good for you after you are done, while in the middle of it you might want to give up.

Tool 4: Share Your Spiritual Path with Others

One criteria for articulating a goal is a willingness to share it with others. You don't need to put it on Facebook or hold a press conference, but it is good to share it with people who are closest to you. Help them understand why you chose the goals you have and what was in your Ignatian imagination. In doing so, you share your faith, including the challenges and the fullness, and make it safe for them to do the same. Sharing your Spiritual Path plan can be an exercise in humility through which you see you don't have all the answers for how to reach your goals. Don't be afraid to ask for help. Community comes from holding on to others.

Call it grace or call it karma, but it really is true that the universe opens up when we share our hearts' desires. When I first offered the Spiritual Path retreat to members of my own faith community and shared with them that I had a desire to offer it to others, one of the participants told the director of a retreat house, and he contacted me! I never would have initiated the connection.

One of the key groups to share your goals with are your stakeholders—those who have a stake in your walking this spiritual path, growing closer to God, and fulfilling your call. It may be scary, but chances are you will receive affirmation and support for your goals if loved ones closest to you see how this process gives you energy. My husband and children are key stakeholders in my life. There is no way I would have completed a single journey without their encouragement and support for reaching my Spiritual Path goals. They were often the fellow pilgrims I needed when that spirit *not* of God was louder than the voice of my Walking Partner. In my work relationships, all of my associates were key stakeholders, so it was vital that I share with them my Spiritual Path work goals. Ask your key stakeholders for support even in small, practical ways. They love you. They get you. They will have your back.

Use caution, however, sharing with those who are the focus of your goals. You don't want them to feel as if they are one of your projects, or as if you are determined to get them to change. Remember this process is about *your* growth, not theirs. For example, sharing with my husband my goals for our marriage helped him recognize the ways I was trying to grow, and allowed him to speak into my goals from a place of gratitude and what he really needed of me.

Sharing your Spiritual Path takes advantage of the grace of networking. Find a partner who shares your goals. You don't have to co-labor alone. You never know—others may be called to the same goal! People who love you, and even people who don't know you very well, will be won over by your passion. They will want to help if they can. Trust that God works through anyone who wills your good. Countless stories have been told of how an invitation came at just the right time. God often works through people who are open to being used in this way. When a friend of mine mentioned to a priest that he struggled with finding a way to use discarded company computers, the priest simply asked, "What about Africa?" That one question opened a floodgate in his heart that led to a new nonprofit organization, time spent living in Africa, and the joy of seeing more than sixty schools blessed with the gift of technology!

Sharing your goals also helps you articulate them in such a way that you are able to better believe in them—in yourself—and are more prepared to be held accountable to them. It wasn't until I articulated *I am a writer* that I began to believe it. At the same time, there is a sense of accountability when you tell someone you will do something. They will ask you how it is going the next time they see you, and you had better be able to give an accounting of yourself! Sometimes I write primarily because I know my husband is going to ask how the writing went today. This accountability is healthy and motivating. The people who are cheering you on are the Spirit of God in human form, here to motivate you when doubts and anxieties set in.

Colloquy 31: Sharing My Spiritual Path Plan

Brainstorm a list of people who have gifts and talents related to my goals and can help me keep walking my Spiritual Path plan.

Would my Walking Partner add anyone else to my list?

Tool 5: Set Up a Personal Board of Directors

Imagine you are a nonprofit with the mission of being a clear reflection of the presence of God in this world as only you can. This nonprofit needs a board of directors who believe in this mission but aren't going to benefit from it other than experiencing the joy of walking this journey with you. These are people who don't have a personal stake in any of your goals but who want what is best for you in terms of your wholeness and connection to God. They are the people who inspire your faith journey, who ask you the tough questions and share your spiritual wavelength. This is the place for mentors and others you trust who are separate enough from your life that whether you reach your goal or not, they will not be personally impacted in any way. Their role is to speak the truth into your journey. Find three of them to be on your board. Their wisdom and intentional presence will help you be accountable to your path. Once a quarter, that is, four times a year, invite these people to dinner with the explicit purpose of sharing an update on your Spiritual Path and asking for their wisdom and insights about your challenges. This is not a meeting about them and their lives, as the focus is on you and yours.

Tool 6: Break Down Annual Goals into Monthly Goals

Goals can be overwhelming. You are called to some big stuff. Do not let that spirit *not* of God tell you it is too big. Instead, take the coming year one month at a time. You can break the monthly goals down to weekly goals and then break them down even more into daily tasks if it helps you stay on track. Some people are achievers, and they need to know they have accomplished something every day. Others are better at doing things when tasks fit organically into the flow of their lives. Either way, taking a pause at the Spiritual Path Monthly Scenic Overlook is a must! This is the Reflect phase of the Cycle of Growth you have been practicing in the previous month. Here you assess, learn, and adapt your plan to be sure you are growing. If you go more than a month without assessing how far you have come, it is too easy to get off course. Each scenic overlook offers a time to pull out your map, see how much ground you have covered, and determine how far you need to go before the next scenic overlook, when you set your goals for the coming month.

Tool 7: Get a Spiritual Director

One of the original hopes for this book was to open doors for people who want deeper conversations about their faith lives. Spiritual direction can spark conversations about consolation, desolation, callings, and the totality of God's presence in your life. Spiritual direction is a hallmark of Ignatian spirituality and the vast majority of Ignatius's work. He directed all his companions through the *Spiritual Exercises*, taught them how to direct others, and the Society of Jesus grew from there. The Spiritual Path is a baby step toward experiencing the depth offered by the *Spiritual Exercises*, but that is a journey no one can do alone. Trained spiritual directors are well versed in helping to discern the voices competing for your soul. If you expect a trained professional to cut your hair, why would you seek anything less to help guide your soul?

A spiritual director does not tell you what to do or how to pray but rather reflects back to you what they hear and see in your reflections about how God is active or distant in your life. Once a month I sit for an hour with my spiritual director, a Sister of Mercy, whom I literally trust with my soul. We talk about my prayer practice, what invitations I am discerning, where I find God, and where I feel lost. Spiritual direction is not therapy. It is about learning to recognize the voice of the Spirit of God and how to be aware of my temptations and weaknesses to the spirit *not* of God.

Having a spiritual director present for your Spiritual Path journey is like having a park ranger waiting for you each month at your scenic overlook to be sure you got there safely. They can offer first aid for the journey, listen to all the amazing things you saw and experienced during the journey, and warn you about the weather forecast for the next segment you are venturing into. He or she may help you understand better some of the things your Walking Partner is trying to get you to see, as well as those things you might have missed.

Tool 8: Post My Plan Where I Will See It Often

Advertisers live by the rule that seven interactions with a potential customer are required before they expect a response. *Seven!* If you spend today discerning this plan and then put it back on the shelf or somewhere in the inbox, the odds of walking this path in the coming year are close to zero. Don't expect God to magically make this happen; you are the co-laborer here. Given the efforts of the spirit *not* of God to deter you from this path, you must be resolute about walking this path and integrating it into your life. Post your plan clearly where you can see it. Separate out the parts of your plan where you need to see them. Put Signposts on your car steering wheel, your coffee maker, or your bathroom mirror. Make your Sacred Mantra your screensaver. Post your goals and monthly steps on your refrigerator for all to see. Many people struggle to find God in their lives, and yet you have been given a map of where God is and how you might get closer. The divine is in the deepest desires of your heart, your relationships, your Signposts, your Sacred Mantra, and each of your goals. Post those sacred words of your Spiritual Path plan where you will be reminded to live into them daily.

Tool 9: Fight Through

I am amazed at how St. Ignatius was so far ahead of his time. What many life coaches today call techniques for success, Ignatius would call spiritual practices. The difference is that he recognized the presence of a Higher Power, not just the brain or human ego, working within them. One of those parallels is how people form new habits. Tom Bartow, author and business coach, developed three phases of habit formation.[48] The first phase he calls "The Honeymoon"—basically those first two weeks after the New Year when we are motivated by the newness of our commitment to change. The second phase is "The Fight Through," when the fun has worn off and old habits start to look more comforting. Finally comes the third phase, when new habits become "Second Nature"—almost. Ignatius coached those doing the Spiritual Exercises through each of these stages almost five hundred years ago!

The Honeymoon phase is similar to the Fourth Week of the Spiritual Exercises when the retreatant contemplates the Resurrection and, having come through their own challenges in discernment of what path to follow in life, emerge with a euphoria to walk with Christ to the ends of the earth. If only we could bottle our spirits during this time! We can savor it, observe it, learn from it, and commit the experience of it to our memories. This euphoria of being called to a spiritual path is very real and life-giving. This spiritual memory is needed to get through the other phases. Savor the first Honeymoon stage right when you make your Spiritual Path plan.

For Bartow, the key to successfully forming new habits is to win at least two to three Fight Throughs. Choose the new habit even when you don't want to. The Ignatian advantage is how you win the Fight Through. First, Bartow coaches you to recognize when you have entered this stage and your need to win it. Similarly, Ignatius taught self-awareness of internal movements and recognition of resistance to a task you thought you were called to do.

Bartow then says to ask two questions: *How will I feel if I do this?* and *How will I feel if I don't do this?* Hundreds of years ago, Ignatius guided his directees to discern the Spirits within them by first looking down one pathway and observing how that made them feel. They then looked down the other pathway and observed how the Spirit moved them on that path. In his translation of St. Ignatius's *Spiritual Exercises*, author David Fleming, SJ, writes, "Clearly place before my mind what it is I want to decide about. Try to be like a balance at equilibrium without leaning to either side. My end is always clearly before me" (*Spiritual Exercises*, no. 179).[49] This reflection can be done in a very short time. I am invited to do something. What will I feel if I do it? What will I feel if I *don't* do it? Am I giving up on this path?

Finally, Bartow says that in order to win a Fight Through or not give up on your habit, do a Life Projection where you imagine how your life will be in five years. This is Ignatian wisdom in business-coaching attire. Recall the Death Bed meditation, "If I were at the moment of my death and so I would have the freedom and clarity of time, what would be the decision I would have made now?" (*Spiritual Exercises*, no. 186) and the advice-to-a-friend meditation, "I observe the advice [in this same situation] which I would so readily give to another for whom I want the best" (*Spiritual Exercises*, no. 185).[50] Bring these reflections to mind to win a Fight Through. You are not being forced to do anything you don't want to do. You are, however, reinforcing your ultimate desire over the immediate ones.

Winning a Fight Through, taking the next step, not giving up on your spiritual path when it gets arduous, is to win a fight with the spirit *not* of God. These fights will arrive in seemingly insignificant moments, like not wanting to get out of bed, or in recurring temptations to throw it all away. Fight through! Your life, your calling, your relationships, and your soul are worth fighting for.

When the road seems too long, your Higher Power asks only that you take the next step today, for tomorrow will worry about itself (see Matthew 6:34).

The third stage of forming healthy habits according to Bartow is when the action feels like second nature to you. But even when your actions no longer require a battle of wills, there can be outside forces that require us to fight through any given day. One danger of this stage is not realizing that your spiritual path is a daily calling that you must commit to one day at a time. The excuse of "I did that for three days straight so I can take a break" is shorthand for "I don't believe this is moving me toward where I need to go." In Alcoholics Anonymous, members can be sober for years, even decades, and still need to attend regular meetings because they are just as close to their next drink as they were the day they started sobriety. Becoming complacent is another tactic of that spirit *not* of God. Don't expect this to be an easy path to follow. Don't expect the spirit *not* of God to give up on luring you into desolation or false consolation. In fact, the closer you get to your calling, the more challenging this fight can become.

Tool 10: Practice Gratitude

The Roman orator Cicero is said to have claimed, "Gratitude is not only the greatest of virtues, but the parent of all the others." St. Ignatius's instructions for the daily *examen* include tapping into gratitude both at the beginning and at the end of each prayer session. If you consider giving up on your Spiritual Path plan or any of your heart's desires, the immediate antidote to that temptation is offering gratitude for the desire itself, or for the journey, or for the joy and hope that lie within that desire, or for the people you have met along the way, and for how these desires have shaped you. These desires of your heart are a unique gift that you and your Walking Partner share. The Spirit of God has seeded them in you. At times you may think they are a curse—*Why can't I just be normal and not care about . . .?* You may be challenged by the sacrifice you are called to make to walk this spiritual path and bring that desire to life. This is what Jesuits mean when they say they are ruined by faith. But, like Mary, regardless of the sacrifice, when you recognize that this heart's desire is divine, you rejoice in being the person chosen to bring it to life. You are the person chosen for these relationships to which you have been called. Gratitude for this calling will always bring you back to connection with your Higher Power.

In the Gospel story of the lepers who were cured by Jesus, ten were made clean but only one returned to thank Jesus. The cleansing or relief of this burden happened "*as they went*," not instantly (Luke 17:14). Everyone seeking to walk a spiritual path is burdened by some barrier to being whole. As you go, month after month, you will find relief from your burdens and gain affirmation of the desires on your heart. Don't forget to go back and say "thank you" along the way.

Tool 11: Seek Grace

In intercessory prayer, such as praying for safety or health, we ask God to do the work. As co-laborers, we are agreeing that we will do the work before us, although we are aware that we need God's Spirit within to do it. Grace goes to the heart of being self-aware and recognizing what we most need in any given situation. Often just in the naming of a specific grace, it is given to us. Seeking grace is the most powerful tool for staying on your spiritual path.

The following aren't the only gifts of the Spirit, so feel free to name any others you are seeking, but these are a good place to start.

- Wisdom
- Understanding
- Counsel
- Fortitude
- Knowledge
- Piety/Humility
- Awe
- Courage—bravery and valor
- Temperance—self-control and restraint
- Generosity
- Joy
- Calm
- Friendliness
- Truthfulness
- Sense of humor
- Fidelity—camaraderie and companionship
- Justice—fairness

Praying for any of these graces is where the Spirit of God meets the vacuum in your soul. You may prefer to put your petition for grace in your own words, as in *Dear God, give me faith to believe you are with me.* Or, *Dear God, give me persistence to never give up on this dream.* Expect and trust that your Walking Partner is carrying the load with you and offers these tools to sustain you.

For what then shall we pray?

Colloquy 32: Naming the Grace Desired to Walk My Spiritual Path

What grace do I most desire in order to walk this path?

My Walking Partner's response:

Naming the grace you need completes your Spiritual Path plan. It is the one tool every pilgrim must use throughout the journey. Complete your Spiritual Path plan by writing the grace you desire on the final blank page of your plan.

What Tools Do I Have the Courage to Use?

We have looked at several different tools to help you stay on your spiritual path. Are there others you think would work for you? Contemplate the ways you can ensure staying on your spiritual path. Use the space below to write down the tools you have the courage or curiosity to use, and share them in the colloquy with your Walking Partner.

Colloquy 33: Tools I Will Use to Stay on My Spiritual Path

Tool 1: Breathe

Tool 2: Practice God-Time Management

Tool 3: The Daily *Examen*

Tool 4: Share My Spiritual Path with Others

Tool 5: Set Up a Personal Board of Directors

Tool 6: Break Down Long-Term Goals into Monthly Goals

Tool 7: Get a Spiritual Director

Tool 8: Post My Plan Where I Will See It Often

Tool 9: Fight Through

Tool 10: Practice Gratitude

Tool 11: Seek Grace

Other Tools That Work for Me:

My Walking Partner's response:

Complete the Cycle of Growth

Using these tools in the first month and reflecting on their impact at the first scenic overlook will complete the Cycle of Growth.

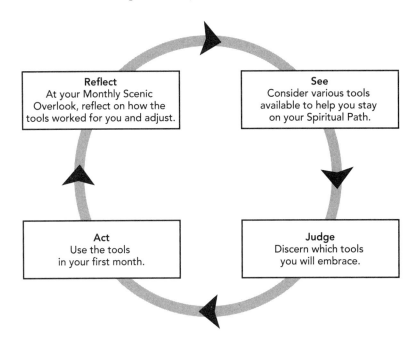

Chapter 12

What's around the Bend?

The Journey of a Lifetime

The goal in sacred stories is always to come back home,
after getting the protagonist to leave home in the first place!
RICHARD ROHR, OFM, *FALLING UPWARD*

Your La Storta

Sixteen years after his initial conversion, Ignatius came to a town in Italy called La Storta, which means "bend in the road." He stopped there to pray in a chapel before meeting the pope in Rome. Ignatius's intention was to ask for papal permission to form a religious order. While in the chapel, Ignatius begged to be placed with God's son. According to George Ganss, SJ, "To be 'with Christ'" meant to be "in close association with him—that had long been Ignatius' ardent prayer." In his colloquy, he heard in response, "I will be favorable to you in Rome."[51] And, indeed, the pope granted his request to begin the Society of Jesus.

This chapter is your La Storta. It reveals a bit of what is around the bend for you in living your Spiritual Path plan over the next twelve months. I have no doubt that God will be favorable to you as well.

Take the Next Step

Sometimes you are called to something, but you have no idea how to get there. God is asking you right now to just take the next step. *Trust me. It won't hurt. I am with you. You can do this. And most of all, no matter what, you are loved.* You don't have to complete your goal all at once. Allow yourself to grow into your goal. Take a step with your Walking Partner, and observe the joy, excitement, energy, and feeling of freedom as you make your way toward your heart's desire. All you have to do is take each next step.

Goals, Objectives, and Tactics

In the corporate world, annual goals are broken down into objectives, and objectives into tactics. Objectives are the ways you reach the goal. Often you need to work more than one front at a time to reach a goal. For example, to be living in a new house by this time next year, you must both find the new house and sell the current one. Or to be reading a book on the shores of Waikiki, you must save money, plan the trip, and make arrangements for your responsibilities to be covered while you're away. Having multiple objectives is the reason why juggling too many goals at once doesn't work. Ten goals with two or three objectives for each means you could be juggling between twenty and thirty different objectives!

Tactics are the specific tasks you need to complete to reach your objective. So to continue our examples, to sell the house you may need to repaint the bathroom, fix the broken downspout, and clear out all the clutter. Tactics are often one and done, while objectives have many tactics within them. Countless hours of consultant time have been spent debating the differences between objectives and tactics. Some people want to get deep into the weeds to have a detailed step-by-step plan for how they are going to get something done. They want to identify the tactics for their tactics. Other people are comfortable simply naming the objective or delegating the objective and supervising the methodology. Resist the temptation to dive too far into the details; don't overplan the journey. As they say, the devil is in the details. It is so tempting to try to control a plan or a relationship. It is too easy to make the tactic or the objective the focus of our attention and lose sight of the original goal. Ignatius had a goal of serving God, with an objective of getting to the Holy Land, but along the way he almost killed a man, which would not have helped to achieve his goal! The consolations and desolations you will experience on your daily journey, while completing the tactics and meeting these objectives, are the basis for your relationship with your Walking Partner. You will experience a sense of joy when you move closer to your goal, continue learning about yourself, overcome challenges, meet new people, and complete your tactics and objectives along the way. The Spirit of God is at work in the process.

Ignatian Wisdom for the Journey

St. Ignatius advises us to be indifferent to our goals. *What?* We just spent thirty-three colloquies discerning a unique spiritual path, and Ignatius wants us to be *indifferent* to it?

For Ignatius, indifference is not the same as apathy. It is non-attachment, a willingness to be flexible and adapt. It calls one to remember the ultimate goal, which has been laid out in the Principle and Foundation. Ignatius said he hoped it would take only fifteen minutes in prayer to give up his Society of Jesus (which he had spent twenty-plus years leading) if it was God's will—and that is an example of indifference according to St. Ignatius. He hoped that he could be indifferent enough to his brainchild, his passion project, his purpose-driven profession, if he discerned that it was God's will that he do so.

When I received my cancer diagnosis, I had to let go of some goals such as learning Spanish fluently. I had to discern new goals for whatever time I had left to me—goals like planning my funeral. Some goals stayed the same. Having a clearly articulated plan helped me so much in continuing to move forward with God and not waste time wallowing in despair about what I didn't get to do. As far as I was concerned, I still had some growing to do, some self-care to put into play, and some relationship building with others. These are the goals I allowed myself to concentrate on.

Making adaptations to your plan is a sign of growth, not of failure! Freedom is always yours to discern what is really primary in your life. If after a month of walking this path you feel more desolate or further from God, then you have the freedom to make adjustments and adapt the plan as you see fit. Change the method, not the goal. I had a goal of practicing centering prayer for twenty minutes a day, but I just couldn't get rid of my monkey mind. Then I did as Ignatius suggested and changed my prayer posture from seated to child's pose. This simple adaptation drew me more deeply into the peace for which I yearned. Anything you try is an opportunity to learn and grow even if you don't achieve the original outcome you hoped for or expected. On the spiritual path nothing is wasted.

Let the pilgrimage unfold before you. Let your Walking Partner surprise you. Ignatius never could have thought that five hundred years after the founding of the Jesuits they would be the largest order of priests and globally provide schools, social services, and churches.

I Have No Idea What to Do

I grew up in a family notorious for not being able to make decisions. Everyone had a different opinion on what to do, and if we did agree on something, there were multiple options on how and when to do it. Going out to dinner was a major affair that stressed everyone out to the point of not wanting to go. One memorable vacation, the stress of deciding what to do led to my father saying out of pure frustration, "Can we please do *something*, even if it's *wrong*?" This became our family mantra. Do not let indecision, which comes from the spirit *not* of God, stop you from acting on your heart's desires. My spiritual director reminds me that short of something immoral, there is no wrong here. There is movement and discernment, there is constant growth, as long as you are intentional and not living a life of being chronically disengaged.

If you truly don't know what the next step is, ask others for their input. Again, from Edward Kinerk, SJ, "As Jesuits we believe that our most authentic desires will be discovered and fulfilled only through collaboration [with others]."[52] If you have no idea where to begin with a goal, talk to twenty people about what they think you should do, and discern the best option by the end of the month. Break that down to one person's input per day. Seek out experts in the arena of your heart's desire to benefit from their wisdom. Not only does that give you clarity about your goal but it also brings others onto your support team. This request honors their wisdom and the divine in them and reminds you that you are not alone on this journey. Have you ever asked a stranger for advice? It can be an amazing conversation starter. Most people are genuinely good at heart and want to help you.

Planning Next Month's Steps

You are ready to go under the banner of your Sacred Mantra. Each month offers a Cycle of Growth. The Cycle begins here as you *see* the possible objectives for reaching each annual or six-month goal. You then *judge* how to progress toward that horizon in the coming month. One month from now, what do you want to have accomplished on this journey? How much time and effort are reasonable, given your other commitments and life events? Perhaps freeing up your schedule is the best first step. Set monthly steps that are ambitious and different from your daily situation, but not so ambitious that you set yourself up for failure. Is there an 80 percent chance you can make this happen with intentionality? "With intentionality" here is short for "with the Spirit of God in my corner." No magic. Nothing in the world around you has changed. You have changed. You have a new Sacred Mantra and some clarity, and you have a Walking Partner.

One fellow pilgrim had a goal to work out at the gym three times a week before work. Getting out of bed was going to be a difficult hurdle for her. Her first month's step was to get out of bed every morning at five. Getting to the gym and doing the workout was a different challenge. By altering her schedule consistently, she made that challenge easier. In one month, she proved to herself she could get up at 5:00 a.m. not just three days a week, but every day. Set yourself up for success and be wary of how ambitious you are at any one time.

The steps to achieve in the coming month can be articulated as a mini-goal (state of being) or as an objective or tactic (action, to-do).

Being able to do something consistently may seem like splitting hairs when compared with *just doing* something, but progress on the journey is easier to see when *you* have changed along the way, not just changed what you have done. For some people, motivation is in the vision. For other people, the motivation is checking off a daily task. Which kind of person are you?

Below is an example of a Monthly Scenic Overlook plan.

My April Spiritual Path Monthly Scenic Overlook

Signposts How well did I follow this Signpost?	Score	Lesson learned/notes/impact/ consolations/desolations
Plan the good stuff!		
Savor *every* opportunity to be a mother!		
Let people be who they are.		
Sacred Mantra	Score	
I share my *truth* with confidence.		
Did I utilize my Sources of Energy?	Yes/No	
Connectedness, positivity, and balance.		
Relationship: (Greatest Invitation for Growth) God's Scribe		
Goal 1: Book is submitted to a publisher by August.	Score	
Steps this month:		
• Integrate retreat feedback.		
• Attend workshop.		
• Line up and prep for readers.		
Relationship: Mother and Imparter of Wisdom to Lem, Andrew, Michael, and Cate		
Goal 2: Have family dinner at least four nights a week.	Score	
Steps this month:		
• Plan meals and shop by Monday p.m.		
• Plan and host family party for Tom.		
Relationship: Mom's Caretaker and Companion in her final years.		
Goal 3: Take Mom out or have her over at least once a week.	Score	
Steps this month:		
• Take a weekend getaway!		
• Take Mom to upcoming doctor appointments and lunch out afterwards.		

Relationship: Community Builder		
Goal 4: Be able to have a basic conversation in Spanish.	Score	
Steps this month:		
• Listen to Spanish podcast five days a week.		
Relationship: Tom's soulmate		
Goal 5: Daily depth, reflection, and laughter with Tom		
Steps this month:		
• Walk dog together three times a week.		
• Leave notes in his bag for his trip.		
Relationship: Tom's soulmate		
Goal 6: Sell house and move to Spain!	Score	
Steps this month:		
• Basement cleaned out.		
Relationship: Protector of my body		
Goal 7: Maintain BMI	Score	
Steps this month:		
• Swim, elliptical, body pump, repeat.		
• Walk dog daily.		
Relationship: My Daily Homies		
Goal 8: Each member of the team achieves their personal goals.	Score	
Steps this month:		
• Plan and bring in lunch for bi-weekly team check in.		

Relationship: God's Scribe		
Goal 9: Have one blog published each month.	Score	
Steps this month:		
• Blog post "Shoes of a Pilgrim" submitted and published.		
Relationship: Justice Advocate		
Goal 10: I remain in solidarity with Mahamed as he integrates into society.		
Steps this month:		
• Attend Mahamed's hearing.		

The Monthly Scenic Overlook includes revisiting your Signposts, Sacred Mantra, and Sources of Energy. These will stay the same each month.

Colloquy 34 prompts you to complete a Monthly Scenic Overlook, that is, imagine, discern, write, and commit to where you will be by the end of the month. You are completing the See, Judge, and Act Cycle of Growth in a continuing colloquy with your Walking Partner. A blank Monthly Scenic Overlook template is provided on pages 219 through 221 for you to make copies of and use to handwrite your steps for each month. A downloadable, fillable PDF can also be found at LaStorta.org/SpiritualPath. To access a digital goal-tracking tool that reflects the structure of your Spiritual Path plan go to bestyearyet.com. To use the blank Monthly Scenic Overlook template in the back of the book or in Colloquy 34, fill in the downward spiral of the plan and your relationship names and goals on the first column before you identify your action steps for the coming month. You can then make copies of this template for each month. Once you write and recommit to the downward spiral of the path, prayerfully go through your goals, starting with your Greatest Invitation for Growth. For now, focus on setting the steps you want to take during the next thirty days by listing them in the first column. You may need multiple steps to progress in the coming month. The Scoring and Lesson Learned columns are explained after you set your monthly steps. Regardless of what tool you use, remember that setting your monthly steps requires a colloquy to include your Walking Partner in the process.

Colloquy 34: Setting the Steps of My First Month

With my Walking Partner, complete this thought for each Spiritual Path goal and write the steps on the first Monthly Scenic Overlook in the back of the book or below: *By the end of this month, I will be or I will have done the following:*

Spiritual Path Scenic Overlook

Month _____

Scoring Guide:

- 0–20% No action or minimal action taken toward this goal.
- 21–40% Some action taken, but not enough to warrant growth toward goal.
- 41–60% Some action taken, some growth or progress made, but not enough to take the next step.
- 61–80% Significant effort and progress. Likely needing to continue into the next month.
- 81–100% Mission accomplished! Sufficient to identify next steps and celebrate!

Signposts How well did I follow my Signpost?	Score	Lesson learned/notes/impact/consolations/desolations
Sacred Mantra Did I utilize my Sources of Energy?	Score	
	Yes/No	

Relationship: (Greatest Invitation for Growth)		
Goal 1:		
Steps this month:		
•		
•		
Relationship:		
Goal 2:		
Steps this month:		
•		
•		
Relationship:		
Goal 3:		
Steps this month:		
•		
•		
Relationship		
Goal 4:		
Steps this month:		
•		
•		
Relationship:		
Goal 5:		
Steps this month:		
•		
•		

Relationship:		
Goal 6:		
Steps this month:		
•		
•		
Relationship:		
Goal 7:		
Steps this month:		
•		
•		
Relationship:		
Goal 8:		
Steps this month:		
•		
•		
Relationship:		
Goal 9:		
Steps this month:		
•		
•		
Relationship:		
Goal 10:		
Steps this month:		
•		
•		

Act

The premise of this book is to put faith into action. Your plan is written and the steps for the coming month are laid out before you. Now is your time to act. Remember all the tools at your disposal to keep you on your path. Even when you are not specifically working on a step in your plan, your Signposts, Sacred Mantra, and Sources of Energy help guide you. Breathe deeply in gratitude for the journey you share with your Walking Partner. Most of all, *savor* the journey with all its actions, consolations, and desolations that lie within each day.

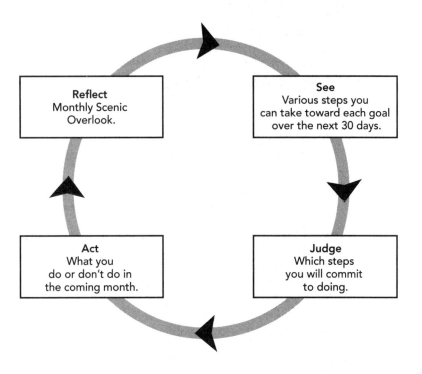

Reflect: The Monthly Scenic Overlook

Put it on your calendar now. One month from now take twenty minutes out of your regular routine to acknowledge and reflect upon the journey of the past thirty days. You can use the same page you just completed to score and learn from the actions taken or not taken during the month. Then set the steps for the next month on another Monthly Scenic Overlook page.

The Monthly Scenic Overlook is also your deadline for action you have discerned. We all need deadlines. Some people see deadlines as motivators, while others see deadlines as monsters. The fact is, you are going to act in some way over the coming days and months. You are going to spend your time doing *something*. The Monthly Scenic Overlook is your opportunity to acknowledge and learn from how you spent your time. Some pilgrims consider this to be a monthly *examen*. Here we talk about what happened and recognize how we experienced those events and what remains in our heart afterwards. And, as always, we listen to any wisdom from our Walking Partner.

Rating Your Journey

One unique aspect of the Spiritual Path process is combining tools of prayer and colloquies with the tools of strategy and accountability, even to the point of scoring yourself. The format laid out on pages 219 through 221 offers an agenda for your Monthly Scenic Overlook. It includes scoring yourself on how well you followed your Signposts, lived your Sacred Mantra, and, most important, did what you said you were going to do in that month.

Why do you need to rate your journey? First, don't think of this scale as a school grading scale where you need a 90 percent or above to get an A and anything below 60 is failing. Don't think of it as a scale that requires hard and fast data to determine your rating. We use a percentage because it is a human way to translate our internal judgments of a situation to a visible scale. But this is your scale. You know where you want to be at this time. Are you there yet? How close are you? What made you miss the mark? Consider the scoring scale that follows for your Monthly Scenic Overlook.

> **Scoring Scale:**
> - 0–20% No or minimal action taken toward this goal.
> - 21–40% Some action taken, but not enough to warrant growth toward goal.
> - 41–60% Some action taken, some growth or progress made, but not enough to take the next step.
> - 61–80% Significant effort and progress. Likely need to continue into the next month.
> - 81–100% Mission accomplished! Sufficient to identify next steps and celebrate!

As you sit in reflection and review the month, recall the times you lived out new behaviors and the times you did not. The number is your gut measurement. But the key is not so much the number as it is your honesty with yourself. As with all assessments, this monthly acknowledgment is meant to be a learning tool and a celebration tool. If you haven't hit your mark by at least 80 percent, then there is something to learn in the coming month. If you have hit your goal by at least 80 percent, you have reason to celebrate. It feels good to know and name what you have done. This is the key reflection part of our growth cycle. Are you feeling consolation or desolation as you reflect on the past month? Are you moving toward God and wholeness with each step you take, or are you moving more into the fears and ego-centric voices of the spirit *not* of God? Don't punish yourself if you don't reach your steps—learn! It will likely take you several months to get comfortable with setting appropriate objectives or tactics, integrating new routines, and finding your footing on your path.

Resting Together

The Monthly Scenic Overlook is ideal for reviewing with your spiritual director or other pilgrims willing to share their own journey with you. In fact, one of my inspirations for translating this process from a corporate planning tool into a spiritual/growth-focused tool was to help give structure to spiritual direction and faith-sharing opportunities. In my experience, these meetings often regurgitate what is happening in our daily lives rather than see daily life as an ongoing journey of growth toward wholeness. The best spiritual directors guide us to focus on growth toward union with God and toward recognition and awareness of our own belovedness.

Alternatively, if you don't have a spiritual director, your monthly reflection is most powerful when shared with other pilgrims who are sharing their journey with you. These people don't have a stake in your plan other than wanting to see you more fulfilled. They are your cheerleaders, your support system, your earth angels. They provide a safe space to reflect and articulate how your journey is going. Ideally, each person completes the Monthly Scenic Overlook and scores their month, then shares their celebrations and lessons learned so others in the group can celebrate and contribute to their reflection. I am dedicated to my path more deeply when I see others act out of their faith and share their experiences of consolation and desolation. This trusted group of fellow pilgrims can be one of the greatest consolations on the spiritual path.

Seasonal Reflections

As you look back each month to learn from the previous leg of your journey and look ahead to the next bend in the road (the next monthly reflection), it can help to stop and take in the larger view. How far have you come this year? How far do you have yet to go? The calendar year is divided into four seasons, roughly three months each, in which the environment around us changes, requiring us to adapt. Every three months, as part of the three-, six-, and nine-month reflection, add in some time to savor this seasonal change and reconnect with the original invitations of your Spiritual Path. You may be surprised how far you have come in just three months. You may make some honest admissions about how the journey is going so far.

At your first Monthly Scenic Overlook, once you have a sense of what is possible, it is helpful to lay out benchmarks for where you want and need to be by the seasonal reflection. Each of these benchmarks delineates a smaller bite of the "Big, Hairy, Audacious Goal" to which you felt called. These are not written in stone. Chances are you will adjust this benchmark, given what you learn in the coming months. A shorter-term marker relieves the pressure of a larger goal and provides a guaranteed reflection point for learning whether adjustments are needed to meet other benchmarks, all the way to the final goal.

The seasonal reflection is not confession or "come to Jesus" time. Your Walking Partner has been with you all along. These quarterly check-ins ensure that the spirit *not* of God is not tempting you to procrastinate or veer off course. It is a chance to look at each area of growth and honestly answer whether or not you are on track and moving at the right pace to be where you want to be by the end of the plan year. If so, reaffirm what you have done and continue on this pace. If not, how can more progress be made in this goal area? Ignatius teaches that places where we don't feel growth toward God are the places where we need to intensify our efforts even more. If one of your relationships causes you desolation, make a special effort to reconnect with that person. Growth does not occur in avoidance. The seasonal reflection offers an opportunity to get back on the path and pick up the pace toward your goal.

Rerouting Your Spiritual Path

As you start to get into the weeds of this Spiritual Path plan, you are free to admit you overreached. You can always discern what is truly primary in your life with more insight and information. Ignatian indifference implores you to not be too attached to any one goal but rather to listen to the movement of your heart as you walk your path. One of the beautiful things about drafting a Spiritual Path plan is that as you learn and grow over the year, you have a path to discern rather than living a reactive, limiting spirituality. If one goal decreases while another increases, you have a document to clearly track that change in desired outcome. You can see where you were six months ago, and where you are heading now. There may be invitations to new relationships or opportunities to grow that you add to your spiritual path. There may be abrupt changes to your spiritual path that are beyond your control. Caring for my aging parents was always a part of my spiritual path, but when my father died and Mom chose to move back to Ohio, my capacity and goals for that relationship had to change. These new situations allow you to assess what invitations still fit your spiritual path. Some aspects may have to go, or the focus may shift and no longer be an option.

There are no rights or wrongs here, only invitations to grow into a deeper experience and union with God through the relationships that define your life. In general, the deepest desires of our heart for wholeness, and the peace that comes from knowing we are using our gifts and capacities to reflect God and be our best selves, don't change drastically month to month or quarter to quarter.

Along the way, whichever way it turns out to be, you can always grow and learn, and perhaps become more comfortable in that new Sacred Mantra you could not have imagined when you first began discerning your spiritual path. Your consolations may free you beyond your greatest expectations. Conversely, this road can be much harder than you ever imagined. Remember the two characteristics of consolation we discussed at the beginning: the sense of wholeness at the time, and the long-term implications or outcome of the action or experience. After you walk this path, you may have a better sense of that long-term outcome as consistent or inconsistent with the sense of consolation you felt in the beginning. In hindsight, you may realize that what you thought was consolation was false and led you away from an opportunity for growth. Adapting the goals, objectives, and tactics of your plan is a sign of growth, not of failure.

The path of St. Ignatius was very different from what he first imagined. He spent months alone, and then in service to others in Manresa, Spain. He attempted to go to Jerusalem, where he was literally thrown outside the gates. Only after that did he realize that he was being called to go back to school. As a result of continuing his education, he found the core group of companions who would share with him his world-changing journey toward God. Even then, the path was more crooked than predictable. He and his companions envisioned a missionary life in the Holy Land; instead, they returned to Europe and began an international education ministry that is still active and influential today. Near the end of his life, Ignatius thought he would travel and share his *Spiritual Exercises* abroad; instead, he spent his final ten years as an administrator in Rome, becoming known as "The Saint at a Desk."

Like Ignatius, you will need to be attentive to the signs of the times and the movements of the Spirit in your life. Be open to altering your path. Trust that everything you have done to get to this point, whatever that point is, is an integral and essential part of the person you are. Refrain from making any adjustments, especially major adjustments in direction, until you have discerned them fully. Don't give up on a goal because it is hard. Fight through for new ways to get there, or at least until a major decision is required of you. Every year or six months you can create a new Spiritual Path plan. The consolations and desolations you notice this year can inform your path for years to come.

What Graces Have I Received through This Process?

I always have some sense of consolation at the end of any hike I have completed. Even if it rained, I made it home and had a story to tell. When you take a hike, your body may be exhausted, but you have reconnected with nature and, maybe, with Something greater than yourself. I hope this Spiritual Path experience has been similar for you. I hope you pushed yourself, explored new territory in your soul, and along the way got closer to your Walking Partner. I hope you recognize that you have clear callings in this life and many more places to go. Your purpose is to praise, reverence, and serve God by being the person you are called to be and are capable of being in this given time and context, and in so doing to save your soul.

The final step in completing the Cycle of Growth is to reflect, acknowledge, and celebrate the entire cycle, the pilgrimage that you have just completed.

To celebrate and acknowledge this journey you have:

- articulated lessons to make your spiritual journey smoother;
- created a Sacred Mantra, a faithful internal compass;
- identified your unique Sources of Energy for this journey;
- discerned your goals and completed a one-page Spiritual Path plan; and
- committed to the first steps on that path over the coming month and the tools you will use to stay on it.

This time we ask not what graces we need but acknowledge what graces we have already received in the process.

- Wisdom
- Understanding
- Counsel
- Fortitude
- Knowledge
- Piety/Humility
- Awe
- Courage
- Self-control and restraint

- Generosity
- Joy
- Calm
- Friendliness
- Truthfulness
- Sense of humor
- Fidelity—camaraderie and companionship
- Justice—fairness

Colloquy 35: What Graces Have I Received?

My Walking Partner's experience of this process with me:

The Journey of Your Lifetime

We are all on a spiritual path whether we write it out or not. We spend each day of our lives doing, learning, acting in ways that form habits and mantras and put us in relationships that shape who we become. God does not have a preset path laid out for you. But God has planted desires in your heart and continually sends invitations through the world and the people around you to join the divine dance. Which invitations will you accept?

We can open our hearts to be touched by God through others and this life, or we can close off our hearts in an attempt to keep them safe. Either way we choose a spiritual path. Our discernments and actions comprise the journey of our lifetime.

In your mind turn to that Walking Partner and repeat your Sacred Mantra.

And listen for the voice of your Walking Partner, who says, "You are my beloved. Let's walk this together."

Gratitude and Acknowledgments

Practitioners of Ignatian spirituality are encouraged to begin and end all things in gratitude. As this mini-retreat concludes and your daily Spiritual Path journey begins, I am rooted in gratitude for you. Thank you for making time to read these words and for being open to the wellspring they might bring to your heart and mind. Very few people take time to discern their responses to the invitations God offers. Whatever time you take to draft and walk your Spiritual Path is a gift not only to yourself, but to the world. By discerning and walking your Spiritual Path, you inspire others to do the same. It may just be the way God desires to work through you today.

I learned the *Your Best Year Yet!* planning process from Karen Morey. Karen has spent the better part of our friendship convincing me that the business world is a world filled with good people, good intentions, good ideas, and good processes. She came to that worldview not from some naive, do-gooder notion that surely everyone else is as big hearted as she is, but from years of experience working with good people in good organizations that are seeking to do good work. Her gift is in coaching them to identify their goals and then following through to make them happen. The *Your Best Year Yet!* planning process that Karen trained me to lead is the brainchild of Jinny Ditzler, a tour de force of the human spirit! Jinny developed and wrote the ten-question process in the 1980s and it has been lauded around the globe for more than forty years by corporations, leaders, students, and coaches, all of whom use those key questions to plan the coming year for themselves individually and for their organizations. Jinny's *Your Best Year Yet!* has sold upwards of 100,000 copies and has been translated into fourteen languages. The *Your Best Year Yet!* (BYY) process is insightful, transformative, simple, powerful, and engaging. Its focus is on "producing results" to achieve your dreams. We all stand on the shoulders of giants. Karen Morey and Jinny Ditzler are mine. Cathey Stamps and Laurie Oswald of Interaworks graciously supported this adaptation in honor of Jinny's legacy.

I am graced by God with several angels who put their own time, heart, and wisdom into this book. Kris Gleason, known as the Passionate Coach, was among the earliest to walk through the retreat with me. Eileen Burke Sullivan, former director of Creighton's Christian Spirituality Program, mentored me through classes. My own faith community of Ignatian Associates was among the first groups to consider the process, and Father Thomas Leitner, OSB, was the first to invite me to offer the Spiritual Path as a retreat at the St. Benedict Center at the Christ the King Priory after Ann Cole recommended it to him. In subsequent years, several retreatants took the leap of faith to be my initial pilgrims, and their feedback and faithfulness was the energy boost I needed. Other spiritual directors, including Ruth and Tim Leacock and Anne Ginn, and fellow writer Alice Smith, reviewed every word of my manuscript and generously contributed their own insights. My own spiritual director, Anne Pellegrino, OSM, graciously put up with years of listening to me talk about the spiritual roller-coaster of being called to write this as a book. Fellow La Storta director, Chris Groscurth, provided significant feedback, enthusiastically participated in the Spiritual Path retreat, and mentored me along the way to publication. Most valiantly, my own personal leadership coach, mentor, dear friend, and fellow director of La Storta, Steve Titus, jumped on board to ensure this work came to fruition. Our conversations about consolation, discernment, goals, and grace were a rare gift in a universe of never-ending tasks.

At Loyola Press, John Christiansen, Vice President of Sales and Marketing, and Gary Jansen, Executive Editor and Director of New Products and Acquisitions, took a total leap of faith to bring this book to the Executive Board for consideration. From day one Maura Poston, as my first book editor ever, knew the exact balance of clarity, criticism, and collaboration. Susan Taylor, copy editor, by far surpassed my fourth grade teacher as the epic standard of grammar in my brain. Carrie Freyer and Liz Emblem brought it home by getting it into your hands. And huge kudos to Donna Antkowiak for somehow understanding literally hundreds of detailed instructions to magically turn this text into book form. There is no need for more proof that living this faith requires a community.

Finally, my husband, Tom Kelly, professor of systematic theology at Creighton University, reviewed, revised, encouraged, and helped me navigate both the spiritual and practical waters of writing this book. He is the one person who has shared my spiritual path since I was eighteen years old. I honestly don't know if he is a better husband or theologian, but I can say he is overwhelmingly good at both.

All of these angels point my ultimate gratitude to my Walking Partner. My consolation is ineffable. Two years ago, I was given twenty-four hours to make a discernment of life or death. My choices were to try a physically brutal, year-long stem-cell transplant or to call hospice. Statistically I am not supposed to be here. I believe through the giftedness of my medical team and cancer researchers, but also through the prayer of a network that literally spans the globe, that I have been carried by my Walking Partner both spiritually and physically.

I live in constant gratitude for my spiritual path, holding each day and invitation sacred. I trust it all leads to the greater glory of God.

The Spiritual Path Daily *Examen*

Plan Date _____ Prayer Date _____

Compose the space. Turn off electronics. Awaken the senses (candles, light music or silence, taste, scents, pillows, posture, vistas).

1. Presence: Greet my Walking Partner as I would when meeting a friend for coffee. Recognize the Spirit they bring me. Wallow in it. Hear, "I am . . . so glad you came." Respond by acknowledging any gratitude I feel.

2. Freedom: Breathe. What do I need to be free of today? Worries, regrets, fears, preoccupations, or stresses? In this space I am safe and loved. Reiterate my Sacred Mantra. Centering Prayer time (optional).

3. Learning/Listening/Daily Reading: Lectio Divina, imaginative prayer, reading aloud, listening to an audio version, or any daily prayer resource.

4. Conscious Review (under the "See" column): What stood out as consoling or desolating on the previous day? See what happened without judgment. Add in any unexpected tasks or events to the Act! column. Note the reality that happened in place of the planned activity, and my feelings and awareness as a result.

Time	Act!			See (No judgment here)	
	Plan		Goal Number /GTM	Reality	Feelings/ Awareness

5. Colloquy: (Judge/Discern)
   Talk/Write with my Walking Partner. Listen! Breathe. Trust. Lessons
   Learned. Movement toward God? Movement away? What caught my
   attention? What distracted me? Journal. Intercessory prayer.

6. Plan (under the Act! column): Together, look toward tomorrow.
   Review Monthly Spiritual Path plan. What are *we* going to do? What
   relationships do *we* need to prioritize tomorrow? Fill in tasks or events
   to the Act! column for the coming day, setting time for those related to
   our goals and relationships first, including the relationship as our own
   caretaker. Note what GTM quadrant each activity would fit into and
   which Spiritual Path goal the activity supports.

God-Time Management	Required (Urgent)	Invited (Not Required)
Engaged (Purposeful, Focused, Intentional)	II. Required and Engaged	I. Invited and Engaged (God Time)
Disengaged (Distracted)	III. Required and Disengaged	IV. Invited and Disengaged

7. Reflect: How has this short prayer time been for us? What grace do I
   seek for tomorrow? What gratitude do I feel?

Spiritual Path Monthly Scenic Overlook

Month _____

Scoring Guide:

- 0–20% No or minimal action taken toward this goal.
- 21–40% Some action taken, but not enough to warrant growth toward goal.
- 41–60% Some action taken, some growth or progress made, but not enough to take the next step.
- 61–80% Significant effort and progress. Likely need to continue into the next month.
- 81–100% Mission accomplished! Sufficient to identify next steps and celebrate!

How well did I follow my Signpost?	Score	Lesson learned/notes/impact/consolations/desolations
Sacred Mantra	Score	
Did I utilize my Sources of Energy?	Yes/No	
Relationship: (Greatest Invitation for Growth)		
Goal 1:	Score	
Steps this month:		
•		
•		
Relationship:		
Goal 2:		
Steps this month:		
•		
•		

Relationship:		
Goal 3:		
Steps this month:		
•		
•		
Relationship:		
Goal 4:		
Steps this month:		
•		
•		
Relationship:		
Goal 5:		
Steps this month:		
•		
•		
Relationship:		
Goal 6:		
Steps this month:		
•		
•		
Relationship:		
Goal 7:		
Steps this month:		
•		
•		
Relationship:		
Goal 8:		
Steps this month:		
•		
•		

Relationship:		
Goal 9:		
Steps this month:		
•		
•		
Relationship:		
Goal 10:		
Steps this month:		
•		
•		

Overall Monthly Reflection\Celebration\Acknowledgments:
What is God inviting me to learn?

Keeping in mind the lessons learned this month, discern with my Walking Partner the steps for the upcoming month on the next Monthly Scenic Overlook.

What grace do I seek for the next part of this journey?

Endnotes

1. Lisa Kelly, "The Shoes of a Pilgrim," *dotMagis Blog* found at Ignatian Spirituality (website), www.ignatianspirituality.com/the-shoes-of-a-pilgrim/.

2. St. Ignatius of Loyola (c. 1491–1556) was the founder of the Jesuits, the largest order of priests and brothers in the Catholic Church.

3. Ignatian Associates are laypersons formed through the Spiritual Exercises who are committed to a life of Simplicity, Apostolic Availability, and Fidelity to the Gospel and our Ignatian and Associate companions. Several Ignatian Associate communities are active across the United States. https://ignatianassociates.org/

4. Jim Collins and Jerry Porras, *Built to Last: Successful Habits of Visionary Companies*, 3rd ed. (New York: Harper Business, 1994).

5. Jim Manney, *What Do You Really Want?: St. Ignatius Loyola and the Art of Discernment* (Huntington, IN: Our Sunday Visitor, 2015), 11.

6. Wilkie Au and Noreen Cannon Au, *The Discerning Heart: Exploring the Christian Path* (Mahwah, NJ: Paulist Press, 2006), 19.

7. T. D. Jakes, *Soar! Build Your Vision from the Ground Up* (Stafford, VA: Faithwork Publishing, 2017).

8. Elizabeth Liebert, *The Way of Discernment: Spiritual Practices for Decision Making* (Louisville, KY: Westminster John Knox Press, 2008), 17.

9. Richard Rohr, OFM, *The Divine Dance: The Trinity and Your Transformation* (New Kensington, PA: Whitaker House, 2016), 204–205.

10. Jinny Ditzler, *Your Best Year Yet!: Ten Questions for Making the Next Twelve Months Your Most Successful Ever* (New York: Grand Central Publishing, 2000), 26.

11. Ditzler, *Your Best Year Yet!*, 30.

12. Stefan Gigacz, "Léon Ollé-Laprune, Philosopher of the See-Judge-Act," October 2001, https://olle-laprune.net/stefan-gigacz-philosopher-of-the-see-judge-act/.

13. Vatican Council II, *Gaudium et spes (Pastoral Constitution on the Church in the Modern World)*, promulgated by Pope Paul VI, December 7, 1965, www.vatican.va/archive/hist_councils/ii_vatican_council/documents/vat-ii_const_19651207_gaudium-et-spes_en.html.

14. Alexandre Borovik, "A Circle with the Center Everywhere," *A Dialogue on Infinity*, April 3, 2008, https://dialinf.wordpress.com/?s=intelligible+sphere&searchbutton=go%21.

15. David L. Fleming, SJ, *Draw Me into Your Friendship: The Spiritual Exercises: A Literal Translation and a Contemporary Reading* (St. Louis, MO: Institute of Jesuit Sources, 2002), 264.

16. Kevin O'Brien, SJ, *The Ignatian Adventure: Experiencing the Spiritual Exercises of St. Ignatius in Daily Life* (Chicago: Loyola Press, 2011), 249.

17. Ruth Leacock, in an interview with the author, Omaha, NE, 2019.

18. Richard Rohr, OFM, *Falling Upward: A Spirituality for the Two Halves of Life* (San Francisco: Jossey-Bass, 2011), 94.

19. Dennis Hamm, SJ, Ignatian Spirituality (website), January 24, 2023, www.ignatianspirituality.com/ignatian-prayer/the-examen/rummaging-for-god-praying-backward-through-your-day/. Reprinted with permission from "Praying Backward through Your Day with the *Examen*," *America*, May 14, 1994, www.americamagazine.org/faith/2023/11/29/vantage-point-dennis-hamm-246604.

20. Ignatius of Loyola, *The Spiritual Exercises*, Third Rule, originally published in his own handwriting, www.ccel.org/ccel/ignatius/exercises.xix.i.html.

21. Fleming, *Draw Me into Your Friendship*, 250.

22. "Introduction to Discernment of Spirits," Ignatian Spirituality (website), www.ignatianspirituality.com/making-good-decisions/discernment-of-spirits/introduction-to-discernment-of-spirits.

23. Richard Rohr, OFM, "Two Kinds of Darkness," Center for Action and Contemplation, https://cac.org/daily-meditations/two-kinds-of-darkness-2017-09-05/.

24. Trails to Wellness, "5 Fs of Trauma Response," Trails (website), www.storage.trailstowellness.org/trails-2/resources/5-fs-of-trauma-response.pdf. Also, All Points North, "Fight, Flight, Freeze, Fawn, and Flop: Responses to Trauma," November 15, 2021, https://apn.com/resources/fight-flight-freeze-fawn-and-flop-responses-to-trauma/.

25. William J. Young, SJ, trans., *St. Ignatius' Own Story: As Told to Luis González De Cámara, With a Sampling of His Letters* (Chicago: Loyola Press, 1956, 1998), 10.

26. Terry Kraus, "Viewpoint: Cunning, Baffling, and Powerful," LinkedIn (website), posted on February 10, 2021, www.linkedin.com/pulse/viewpoint-cunning-baffling-powerful-terry-kraus/. Also, Bill W. and Dr. Bob, *Alcoholics Anonymous: The Story of How Many Thousands of Men and Women Have Recovered from Alcoholism*, 3rd ed. (New York: AA World Services, Inc., 1976), 58.

27. Scott Jeffrey, "The Ultimate List of Core Values," (revised March 27, 2024), www.scottjeffrey.com/core-values-list/#:~:text=In%20no%20particular%20 order%3A%201%20Integrity%202%20Feelings,6%20Creativity%207%20 Freedom%208%20Courage%20More%20items.

28. Tom Rath, *StrengthsFinder 2.0* (Washington, DC: Gallup Press, 2007).

29. Albert L. Winseman, Donald O. Clifton, and Curt Liesveld, *Living Your Strengths: Discover Your God-Given Talents and Inspire Your Community* (Washington, DC: Gallup Press, 2008).

30. E. Edward Kinerk, "Eliciting Great Desires: Their Place in the Spirituality of the Society of Jesus," *Studies in the Spirituality of Jesuits* 16, no. 5 (1984): 19. Published online February 28, 2013, https://ejournals.bc.edu/index.php/jesuit/ article/view/3730.

31. John Reid and Maureen Gallagher, *The Art of Change: Faith, Vision, and Prophetic Planning* (Ligouri, MO: Ligouri Publications, 2009), 18.

32. Fleming, *Draw Me into Your Friendship*, 27.

33. Au and Au, *Discerning Heart*, 137.

34. Gerard Manley Hopkins and Tom Hopkins, *Poems and Prose of Gerard Manley Hopkins* (Norwalk, CT: Easton Press, 2001).

35. Reid and Gallagher, *The Art of Change*, 41.

36. https://friendsofsilence.net/newsletter/september-1996

37. Kinerk, "Eliciting Great Desires," 23.

38. Kinerk, "Eliciting Great Desires," 21.

39. Kinerk, "Eliciting Great Desires," 22.

40. George T. Doran (1981), "There's a S.M.A.R.T. way to write management's goals and objectives" (PDF), *Management Review*, 70 (11): 35–36, November 1981, https://community.mis.temple.edu/mis0855002fall2015/files/2015/10/ S.M.A.R.T-Way-Management-Review.pdf.

41. Irish Jesuits, *Sacred Space for Lent 2016* (Chicago: Loyola Press, 2015), 3.

42. Mark E. Thibodeaux, SJ, *God's Voice Within: The Ignatian Way to Discover God's Will* (Chicago: Loyola Press, 2010), 37.

43. Kinerk, "Eliciting Great Desires," 21.

44. Au and Au, *Discerning Heart*, 138.

45. Thomas Merton, *Thoughts in Solitude* (New York: Farrar, Straus and Giroux, 1999), 79.

46. Stephen R. Covey, *First Things First* (New York: Simon and Schuster, 1994).

47. J. C. Lupis, "How Much Time Do US Adults Spend Watching TV?," Marketing Charts (website), March 14, 2023, www.marketingcharts.com/television/tv-audiences-and-consumption-229018.

48. Selk, Jason. "Habit Formation: The 21-Day Myth," *Forbes Online*, Orig., April 15, 2013, www.forbes.com/sites/jasonselk/2013/04/15/habit-formation-the-21-day-myth/

49. Fleming, *Draw Me Into Your Friendship*, 141.

50. Fleming, *Draw Me Into Your Friendship*, 143.

51. George E. Ganss, SJ, *Ignatius of Loyola: The Spiritual Exercises and Selected Works* (New York: Paulist Press, 1991), 41 and 42.

52. Kinerk, "Eliciting Great Desires," 19.

About the Author

I was given a terminal diagnosis of AITL Lymphoma when I was fifty-two. As I looked back over my life, I suppose doing a literal deathbed meditation, finishing this book was the only thread left untied. I was blessed with four incredible children and a beautiful thirty-plus year marriage to my college sweetheart. As an undergrad at the University of Notre Dame, I studied government and was introduced to the challenges of social justice. I taught high school theology for a few years, but it wasn't until I went to Harvard's Kennedy School of Government that I realized my faith was the primary driver of my worldview. I worked and consulted in government and nonprofit administration, lived abroad with my family, and started a faith-based leadership program. There I was introduced to many different leadership tools used in the corporate world that easily reflected my faith-based worldview but danced around any reference to a Higher Power. Now finishing my Master's in Christian Spirituality from Creighton University (2025), I can write freely that the Spirit does reside in all things, all people, all places, all experiences, and that leadership is not limited to being assigned a role or a certain job. We can all lead with Love in everything we do.

Please feel free to contact me at LaStorta.org.

My Spiritual Path

Dates from _____ to _____

Signposts
   1.
   2.
   3.

My Sacred Mantra

My Sources of Energy
   1.
   2.
   3.

My Greatest Invitation for Growth

My Spiritual Path Goals
   1.
   2.
   3.
   4.
   5.
   6.
   7.
   8.
   9.
  10.

The Grace I Most Desire for Walking This Path